Readers and reviewers offer praise
for the first of Allison Bottke's Setting Boundaries books,
Setting Boundaries with Your Adult Children

"When adult children lose their way, the parents hurt too, especially if the parents don't have clearly defined boundaries. Setting boundaries can be difficult, but in the long run, it prevents untold anxiety, stress, and heartache. Allison Bottke, writing through her own hurt and healing, has compiled a masterpiece of advice. She doesn't just tell you or show you how it's done. She walks along beside you."

Eva Marie Everson and Jessica Everson
authors of *Sex, Lies, and the Media*
and *Sex, Lies, and High School*

"Lack of boundaries with adult children is a worldwide epidemic with catastrophic consequences. Allison not only shares her experience as a parent who has traveled this painful road but also gives readers concrete tools to stop the insanity and start living a life of hope and healing. *Setting Boundaries with Your Adult Children* is destined to be the official resource of hope for countless parents and grandparents."

Heather Gemmen Wilson
author of *Startling Beauty: My Journey
from Rape to Restoration*

"Allison Bottke has stepped forward in a courageous, straight-from-the-heart manner and dealt with an issue that has plagued parents since the dawn of time: setting (and enforcing) boundaries with rebellious adult children. As a parent and a pastor who has faced this issue countless times, I am excited that this mother who has wrestled with demons to see her child delivered has written a heartfelt and practical book of advice and encouragement that will bless each and every person who reads it."

Kathi Macias
author of 20 books, including
Mothers of the Bible Speak to Mothers Today

Setting Boundaries with Your Aging Parents

ALLISON BOTTKE

HARVEST HOUSE PUBLISHERS

EUGENE, OREGON

Published in association with the literary agency of The Steve Laube Agency, LLC, 5025 N. Central Ave., #635, Phoenix, Arizona, 85012.

Cover by Garborg Design Works, Savage, Minnesota

SETTING BOUNDARIES WITH YOUR AGING PARENTS
Copyright © 2010 by Allison Bottke
Published by Harvest House Publishers
Eugene, Oregon 97402
www.harvesthousepublishers.com

Library of Congress Cataloging-in-Publication Data
  Bottke, Allison.
  Setting boundaries with your aging parents / Allison Bottke.
     p. cm.
  Includes bibliographical references.
  ISBN 978-0-7369-2674-4 (pbk.)
  1. Families—Religious aspects—Christianity. 2. Parent and adult child—Religious aspects—Christianity. 3. Adult children—Family relationships. 4 Intergenerational relations—Religious aspects—Christianity. 5. Aging—Religious aspects—Christianity. I. Title.
  BT707.7.B68 2010
  248.8'45—dc22
                                                                              2009047889

Printed in the United States of America

10 11 12 13 14 15 16 17 18 / VP-SK / 10 9 8 7 6 5 4 3 2 1

To my son, Christopher.

You taught me that love can survive
and even thrive when we set boundaries.
You are a walking miracle—a testament
to how God can change a life.
May God use you and your
U-Turn story in a mighty way
to shine light into dark places
and bring hope into empty hearts.

I love you.

You will know the truth,
and the truth will set you free.
JOHN 8:32

Contents

Foreword

by Mark Sichel

In *Setting Boundaries with Your Adult Children*, Allison Bottke candidly described painfully watching her only son self-destruct in a web of addiction and financially destructive behavior. As she explored ways to help him stop this spiral downward, she realized the only ways she could help him were by changing *her own* thinking and behavior and by no longer enabling his addictions. She came to the conclusion that her inability to set appropriate boundaries had perpetuated a dysfunction that was jeopardizing her own health as well as his. She shared with readers what amounted to a fearless personal inventory of her psychological and spiritual world that ultimately allowed her to understand the necessity of boundaries in a close relationship.

Setting Boundaries with Your Aging Parents is written in the same spirit of hope, generosity, and faith that allowed the readers of Allison's first *Setting Boundaries* book to find a sane and safe place of recovery, optimism, and healing. It is an inspiring and important addition to the body of literature that addresses the problem and pain of adult children dealing with difficult parents. I happen to be an expert in this subject, but I am always in need of the collective wisdom shared by a community of survivors.

Allison Bottke adds to each of our efforts to garner hope, wisdom, and support to create lives of loving relationships unclouded by abusive childhoods. Her personal story is gripping and compelling as are the painful stories of any of us who have had to learn new and self-protective behaviors.

In *Setting Boundaries with Your Aging Parents*, the stories of adult children drowning in despair ring true to me because Allison so accurately describes the gut-wrenching agony of adult children doing the right things for their parents and still feeling troubled or abused. I was eventually estranged from my parents when I set a boundary and stopped accepting their abusive behavior. With time I've come to an inner reconciliation that is still often challenged by the cultural belief that family relationships should be protected and sustained at all cost.

My training as a psychologist precluded faith-based solutions to psychological problems. But over time, I've come to reject the scientific dogma rampant in my profession and have incorporated prayer and faith in God in my professional practice and daily life. I realized that when my parents cut off ties with me, my struggles were not only psychological. Rather, and even more importantly, they troubled my soul and made me yearn for faith and trust in God. Allison Bottke's *Setting Boundaries* books offer sound psychological advice that is stunningly integrated with the importance of understanding that God is the ultimate authority who overrides both societal and psychological beliefs.

Residing in New York City, I was nine months into my family estrangement in 2001 when I was challenged to call on all the spiritual resources I could muster to get through the painful and demanding days, weeks, and months that began with the September 11 terrorist attacks. During this time, I learned the importance of the spiritual component in healing of any kind. That day I responded to a call I heard on the local news for mental health volunteers to go to the Red Cross to work with victims of the tragedy. The mayor of New York, Rudy Giuliani, set up a mental-health hotline for the families of victims who needed immediate attention. I spent that night—perhaps the longest night of my life—talking to people who had missing relatives and were still hoping against hope that their loved ones had survived the attack on the World Trade Center. At this point no one had any idea just how few survivors there would be.

That night, I realized my skills as a psychotherapist were all but useless. The only tools I could draw upon were human ones, based on faith. "My prayers are with you and your relative," I said to my callers.

"May God bless you," they replied.

I treated everyone I spoke to with as much kindness and love as I could muster. As the days went on, my fellow New Yorkers and I turned to our most spiritual selves as we mourned as a community and as a family.

Since that time, I have become increasingly convinced that coping with aging parents who are dysfunctional, sometimes financially and psychologically overburdening, and other times downright mean and self-centered is as much a spiritual task as a psychological one.

Right now you may feel as if you're drowning in a pit of confusion, sadness, and perhaps even rage, but I believe that you, like me, will find faith, hope, optimism, and most importantly, sanity as you read through these inspiring pages and chapters on your journey to find peace and serenity in your life.

Mark Sichel
licensed clinical social worker
author of *Healing from Family Rifts:*
Ten Steps to Finding Peace After Being
Cut Off from a Family Member

What This Book Is Really About

The caller was clearly distraught as he asked his question on the nationally syndicated radio program.

"I know your book is for parents and grandparents who are struggling with setting boundaries with their adult children but, what if the situation is reversed? What if the adult children are having boundary struggles with their parents?"

That wasn't the first time I had been asked this question. I address our society's current epidemic of enabling our adult children, so listeners and readers hope I might also have answers for adult children who are dealing with boundary problems with their parents. These unexpected questions formed a pattern from the very start and increased with every interview I conducted. I was about to respond to this caller when he quickly continued.

"My parents have had a tough time this past year. They're getting older, and it's costing more for their medication and other health-care needs not covered by their insurance. I helped them create a budget, and I go to their house and sit down with them every month to review their expenses. I've also been helping them make ends meet by supplementing their monthly income with cash. I've been glad to do this while they get back on their feet."

He did this every month. He worked with them, he budgeted with them, and when there was a shortfall, he paid money out of his own pocket to help his parents. However, they called him that month asking for more money to pay their bills. As it turned out, they'd been giving their own money, which was allocated to pay their bills, to their daughter (his sister) to help her out during a financial crisis. In further discussion, he disclosed that his sister lives far beyond her means and also has drug and alcohol problems. Now, his parents are helping her with their money, he is still helping them with his money, and he was truly perplexed.

"It will never stop. She'll bleed them dry. I agreed to help them, not to enable my sister's drug habit. I can't afford to financially support myself and pay all of my parents' expenses forever. What should I do?"

I could tell by the tone of his voice that he was in anguish. He wanted to be able to help his aging parents, but he clearly felt conflicted about this turn of events.

On the heels of this call came another.

"My parents divorced several years ago after many years of marriage, and my husband and I have been helping Mom pay her rent. Well, she now has a new boyfriend, and we're okay with that—in fact, we're happy for her. But he's moved in with her, he's not working, and he does nothing to help with the bills, the house, the yard…nothing. So here we are, paying rent for my mom and her live-in boyfriend, and it's causing some challenges. What do we do?"

The situation clearly troubled this caller, and her voice wavered with emotion at several points.

Later that same week, I had another live interview on a different nationally syndicated radio program. We were discussing the Six Steps to SANITY as they pertain to our adult children, and the host opened the program for callers. As typically happens when this hot-button topic is addressed, the phone lines in the studio lit up. This time, however, the scales tipped in the opposite direction, as the majority of the incoming calls were from adult children who wanted advice for setting boundaries with their parents. A young man shared his story with great sadness in his voice.

"My dad is continually borrowing a twenty here, a twenty there. He always says he'll pay me back when he gets his monthly Social Security check, but he never does."

"How often does this happen?" I asked.

"Pretty much every time I see him—once or twice a week maybe. But there's more…"

Indeed there was.

At his father's request, he had bought a car for his father and put it in his name because his father's credit was bad. His father had promised to make the payments. Now, after three months, his father hadn't made a single payment.

"I've been making the payments because the car is in my name and I don't want my credit score to be damaged. I hate to see my 65-year-old dad without a car, but I'm getting married, and this financial burden is causing some stress for my fiancée and me. What should I do?"

Although money seems to be a prevailing issue, the calls aren't always about that. Adult children are concerned about the excessive (and sometimes overbearing) neediness of parents—many who are living independently and are able to care for themselves but nonetheless are leaning heavily on their adult children. The adult children are also concerned about aging parents who stubbornly refuse to take proactive measures to prepare for the future. These adult children live in a nearly constant state of stress because they have to react on the fly to mini-crises related to housing, health care, legal matters, and such. They are heartbroken over rifts with other family members who disagree about how to address these issues. Many are concerned about their changing roles as full- or part-time caregivers and their increased responsibility for many (if not all) areas of their parents' life. The list of concerns goes on, yet their question remains the same: "What should I do?"

Let me begin by saying that I'm not a professional counselor or therapist. I wrote *Setting Boundaries with Your Adult Children* over the course of many years and out of my own pain and heartache. I managed to find sanity in what had become an insane situation with my own son, and I felt compelled to share with other parents and grandparents the Six Steps to SANITY that helped me find hope and healing. Having walked this journey as a mother, I felt comfortable not only talking about it but also listening to stories from other parents—not offering therapeutic advice or professional counsel, but sharing my perception and opinions based on similar experiences.

I never imagined that so many adult children were also experiencing pain and heartache as they struggled to set boundaries with their parents. Yet everywhere I went, I heard stories about parents or grandparents violating boundaries. People asked difficult questions, hoping I could help them find answers.

The enabling of our adult children has become an epidemic in our society with catastrophic consequences, and I have begun to see that another equally damaging affliction is threatening families throughout the country—our inability (or unwillingness) to set healthy and desperately needed boundaries with our parents.

Setting boundaries with our adult children is distinctly different from addressing this issue with our aging parents, especially when our parents have many needs. But the concept of boundaries remains the same—we need to guard our hearts, protect our priorities, and do the right thing.

But what *is* the right thing?

Many adult children are fully capable of taking care of themselves when we establish firm boundaries with them, but this may not always be the case with our aging parents. The elderly gradually lose control of their physical health, motor skills, and mental acuity. They are usually on a fixed income and may be unable to drive. Their loved ones may pass away, and loneliness can set in. These things may seem overwhelming and can foster more and more dependence on an adult child. That's why realistic and workable boundaries need to be put in place.

But what if our aging parents do have control and are able to make independent choices—sometimes *questionable* choices that leave their adult children fighting for their sanity and struggling to determine the right thing to do?

If you have read *Setting Boundaries with Your Adult Children*, you know that it is a personal story. At the writing of this second *Setting Boundaries* book, I have an adult child who is serving a sentence in a state prison in Minnesota. Finding sanity amid the chaos, crisis, and drama that surrounded his life was a difficult journey. Loving my son meant letting him go. When I allowed him to experience the consequences of his choices and actions, I took a significant step in setting healthy boundaries in his life and in mine.

But what do we do when the situation is reversed, when we are the adult children and our aging parents are the ones surrounded by chaos, crisis, and drama? What do we do when their choices and actions hurt them, hurt us, and hurt our families? And even if their choices do cause us pain, how can we let go of those who gave us life, who sacrificed for us when we were children, and whom God commands us to honor?

What should we do when a relationship that God intended to be loving and nurturing becomes filled with resentment, anger, frustration, impatience, confusion, guilt, blame, shame, and depression? What should we do when some of our parents' choices break our hearts and cause us pain? How can we avoid burnout and build mutual respect? Should we ever say no to our parents? How can we maintain our sanity?

I've learned a great deal in my decades-long journey of setting boundaries in my own life and finding sanity in my difficult relationship with my adult son—my only child. I've also gained insight into the world of boundaries as founder of the international SANITY Support Group Network.

Since the release of *Setting Boundaries with Your Adult Children*, countless parents and grandparents around the world have learned to set healthy boundaries using the Six Steps to SANITY. In fact, SANITY support groups are meeting around the world in churches, community centers, businesses, and homes, as well as online, following a 12-week course using these life-transforming steps. These same six steps will be the foundation of every *Setting Boundaries* book.

This isn't another book on elder care. A vast amount of information is already available for full- or part-time caregivers—countless resources to help guide and inform adult children through the labyrinth of concerns associated with this delicate season of life.

Additionally, thanks to the Internet, a huge storehouse of information for caregivers is only a click away. Therefore, I will not spend time reiterating the educated wisdom of professionals who are well-versed on the many issues surrounding the intricate journey of elder care, such as these:

> making decisions for your parents
>
> legal concerns and guardianship
>
> long-distance caregiving
>
> stress among siblings
>
> medical, physical, and emotional challenges
>
> disabilities and handicaps
>
> extended and assisted care
>
> nursing homes
>
> parents who live with you
>
> finances
>
> grief, loss, and mourning
>
> widowhood
>
> terminal illness
>
> hospice care
>
> end-of-life decision making

In this book I focus primarily on situations concerning aging parents who are, for the most part, still in control of their mental faculties—who have not been touched by the ravages of dementia or Alzheimer's, who are cognitively able to make their own decisions and choices. As you can imagine, this is a critical distinction.

Don't get me wrong. Setting healthy boundaries is possible (and highly recommended) even if your parents' mental and emotional capabilities are diminished. But if you are in this situation, you may need an entirely different strategy to find balance and sanity. Such is also the case for parents who desire to set boundaries with adult children who suffer from mental illness, bipolar disorder, or other factors that must be considered when making choices and implementing life-changing boundaries.

So available resources on elder care are plentiful—that is, unless you are experiencing the aging parent issue I will address, in which case your resources are far less extensive.

This book assumes your relationship with your aging parents is not working or is becoming strained. If you long for a better relationship with your parents but feel trapped in their seemingly never-ending cycle of chaos, crisis, or drama, these chapters are for you. If your relationship with your parents is becoming increasingly dysfunctional, or if you're nearing the end of your rope and are feeling a little crazy, read on.

My parents have been gone from this earth many years. I was estranged from my father, and the last time I saw him, I was a teenager. He died years before my sister, my brother, and I were even aware of it. My beloved mother spent the last years of her life in an assisted-living center far from me but only a few miles away from my older sister, who lovingly cared for her as she juggled a full-time job, family, and home.

I would give just about anything to have a "do over with my parents." Alas, that is not an option for me. But perhaps it is for you.

Perhaps your journey from burnout to respect will bring you to a place of hope and healing where a "do over" with your parents can become a reality. Setting healthy boundaries with love and mutual esteem can enhance the remaining years you have with the people who gave you life and raised you to become the person you are today.

Your parents will one day leave this earth. That day may be soon—or not. Your task is to put in motion a plan that will give your parents the quality of life they deserve and keep you from becoming spiritually, emotionally, or financially bankrupt. Reasonable boundaries will help you accomplish this goal and will prevent you from making poor decisions now and feeling guilty for years after your parents are gone.

My prayer is that you will not only find sanity in your life but also rebuild and even strengthen your relationship with your parents, regardless of how strained it may be today.

A Critical Truth

This book addresses more than our growing inability as a society to set healthy boundaries. It's designed to be a ministry tool that will inspire, empower, and equip you to transform your life. The Six Steps to SANITY work and will help you get your life back.

This book explores a critical truth regarding setting boundaries with the people you love: If you're struggling with poor choices your loved ones are making, if you are turned inside out and living from one crisis to the next in pain, fear, anger, or frustration because of their choices, you are probably responding by making some poor choices yourself. Therefore, the primary goal of this book is to help you identify the role you play in your relationship with your aging parents and to help you avoid burnout and build mutual respect.

Sanity is possible, and I want to help you find it.

Our Mission: To deliver hope, healing, freedom, and SANITY to anyone struggling with relationship issues concerning weak or nonexistent personal boundaries.

Our Goal: To share the Six Steps to SANITY with those who desperately need it and to equip them to write a Setting Boundaries Plan of Action that will direct them on the road to SANITY.

Our Prayer: That God will empower people around the world to use the principles of SANITY to make choices that will forever change their lives.

What Is SANITY? Peace of mind and heart! Consider these Six Steps to SANITY as life-saving tools to help you better define and forge healthy boundaries.

> **S**—Stop your own negative behavior.
>
> **A**—Assemble a support group.
>
> **N**—Nip excuses in the bud.
>
> **I**—Implement rules and boundaries.
>
> **T**—Trust your instincts.
>
> **Y**—Yield everything to God.

Visit us online at www.SettingBoundaries.com.

Part One

Avoiding Burnout
and Building Mutual Respect

"I had to reach the end of the line before I could refuel my engine and get back on the tracks of life," said Joe. A retired railroad engineer, he had spent the past decade caring for his aging father—a bitter man who never hid his disdain for his only son.

"I kept hoping he would change—that he would see how much we loved him and maybe lighten up a bit." But he never did. Not even after Joe and Gladys, his wife of 30 years, opened their home to him when his finances and failing health made it difficult for him to live on his own.

"We set him up in his own part of the house. I renovated the two bedrooms at the north end so he had kind of his own apartment—even made an access door to the kitchen for him. We bought him new furniture because his was old. We even moved stuff around in the garage so he could park his car on one side. Gladys kept telling me we had to lay down some rules, but I wouldn't listen to her."

Today, Joe lives by himself in the rambling house. His father moved to an assisted-living home (where he's doing fine), and Gladys moved out six weeks earlier. A divorce seemed imminent.

"She couldn't take it anymore," Joe continued. "I was only trying to help, but I let him walk all over me and my wife. Regardless of what we did for him, it was never good enough. I wasted ten years of my life and lost my marriage because I wanted to show my dad I was responsible, and he couldn't have cared less. I never stood up for what was right, so my wife lost respect for me. I should have listened to her. I hope she'll come back—I was stupid…"

Joe had to experience total burnout before he was able to see the role he played in his dysfunctional relationship with his aging father. He never stood up for what was right. If he had established clear boundaries sooner, his relationships probably would not have been devastated. The outcome could have been much different.

Why We Have Trouble Setting Boundaries

People sometimes view boundaries negatively, as if setting boundaries (especially with parents) implies dishonor, rejection, or selfishness. Nothing could be further from the truth as Henry Cloud and John Townsend share in *Boundaries:*

> For years, Christians have been taught that protecting their spiritual and emotional property is selfish. Yet God is interested in people loving others, and you can't love others unless you have received love inside yourself.
>
> This principle is illustrated when the psalmist says, "Above all else, guard your heart, for it is the wellspring of life" (Proverbs 4:23). When we watch over our hearts (the home of our treasures), we guard them.[1]

We Make Emotional Choices

Another reason we have trouble setting boundaries is that we're too emotionally involved in the situation to consider it objectively. In such cases, we often rely on our feelings rather than thinking the matter through. When possible, we should make choices calmly, rationally, and with prayerful wisdom, especially when they significantly affect our relationships. Unfortunately, many of us often make choices concerning our aging parents based on myths and on emotions like these:

fear	anger	guilt
denial	shame	blame

Why We Do This

We're like gerbils on a wheel, going around and around, seemingly unable to stop the out-of-control habits we've developed. Why do we do this? Here are some reasons:

> We don't understand our place within the family of God.
>
> We've lost sight of our priorities.
>
> We've neglected to define our personal boundaries.
>
> We think we don't have a choice.
>
> Our own destructive patterns get in the way.
>
> We ignore our own health and well-being.

Setting boundaries is a way to protect both parties. It's a way to stay on alert and face problems early on so they won't fester and destroy you, your marriage, or your family. You can and should set boundaries with your aging parents and in-laws about advice, money, phone calls, visits at their house, visits at your house, holidays, vacations, gossip, raising your kids, and the like. Yet too often, we either ignore the warning signs or simply wait passively and let the chips fall where they may because we're afraid of being misunderstood. As a result, we spend our time putting out fires that we could have prevented.

What Is a Boundary?

To discover other people's unique perspectives on setting boundaries and finding balance with aging parents, I've been distributing a questionnaire to men and women around the country for more than a year. I'll refer to the results of this survey throughout the book.

Webster's defines a boundary as "something that marks or fixes a limit…a territory, border, frontier." Issues cause relational pain when boundaries are absent, misdrawn, or abused. Boundaries can bring freedom to you and your family. It's important to know what a boundary is and what it is not.

A Boundary Is…	A Boundary Is Not…
healthy	rejection
necessary	selfish
biblical	sinful
respectful	disrespectful
loving	dishonoring

Our most obvious boundaries are the fences we build around our homes. They clarify where our property begins and ends. They protect what belongs to us. With fences in place, we would not hesitate to speak up if a neighbor drove a tractor into our yard and began to dig up our fruit trees or destroy our lawn. Yet when we don't define our limits and protect our own lives—when we don't guard our hearts—we permit others to destroy something far more valuable than trees and lawns. We permit them to destroy our sanity, our spirit, our self-respect, and our most important relationships.

That's what happened to me until I learned why I had difficulty setting the healthy but intangible boundaries that define the core of who I am. During my journey, I discovered a pivotal book that provided biblical insight. *Boundaries,* by Henry Cloud and John Townsend, is the benchmark resource for Christians who desire biblical wisdom and insight about this issue. I'll refer often to this book. Weak boundaries cause destructive patterns and keep people dysfunctional, and the problem is far more common than we might imagine.

> Any confusion of responsibility and ownership in our lives is a problem of boundaries. Just as homeowners set physical property lines around their land, we need to set mental, physical, emotional, and spiritual boundaries for our lives to help us distinguish what is our responsibility and what isn't. The

inability to set appropriate boundaries at appropriate times with the appropriate people can be very destructive. And this is one of the most serious problems facing Christians today. Many sincere, dedicated believers struggle with tremendous confusion about when it is biblically appropriate to set limits.[2]

Why are we so confused? How did we get to this place?

We'll address those questions and more in the chapters that follow as we take a closer look at how we got here and why we have trouble setting boundaries in the first place.

How can you determine whether you need to establish healthy boundaries? If you answer yes to any of the questions below, you may need to start making some new choices.

Do people take advantage of you?

Do you have trouble saying no?

Do you often feel guilty?

Do you feel as though you have no control over your life?

Do you try to have too much control over your life?

Types of Boundaries

Personal boundaries define who we are and influence all areas of our life. As Cloud and Townsend explain, we have many kinds of boundaries:

physical

mental

emotional

financial

spiritual

Here's a simple example. When I was younger, I loved going to amusement parks and riding the Scrambler, the Tilt-a-Whirl, and the Caterpillar. Yet the older I got, the more these rides made me dizzy. Even worse, they started making me nauseous, sometimes for several hours. Eventually, I had to define a clear physical boundary to protect my body. Regardless of how fun these rides appeared, how many happy memories they had provided, and how much my well-meaning friends coaxed me, I could no longer go on these amusement park rides—period. My physical boundary line had been drawn, and should I cross it, the consequences would be unpleasant, and I would have no one to blame but myself. I knew better.

Am I selfish because I do what is best for me and don't give in to friends who prod, cajole, whine, or get angry with me because I don't accompany them on rides? Have I rejected my friends by not following their requests? Of course not. I've simply set a physical boundary with amusement park rides. I know where my limits are, what is best for me, and when to say no.

Why We Need Boundaries

To begin our journey to avoid burnout and build mutual respect, we must clarify why we need boundaries at all. Quite simply, God has mandated them—this is the way He wants us to live. Cloud and Townsend make it clear:

> The most basic boundary-setting word is no. It lets others know that you exist apart from them and that you are in control of you. Being clear about your no—and your yes—is a theme that runs throughout the Bible (Matthew 5:37; James 5:12).[3]

Healthy boundaries will empower you to take back your life and find sanity. Without them, our lives become unmanageable, and burnout is imminent. There is no sugar-coating this truth.

What Is Burnout?

The term *burnout* originally described the moment jet or rocket engines stopped operating. Herbert Freudenberger and Geraldine

Richelson applied the term to human lives in 1974 in their book *Burn-out: The High Cost of High Achievement*. They defined burnout as "the extinction of motivation or incentive, especially where one's devotion to a cause or relationship fails to produce the desired results."

Many of us are devoted to our parents, yet regardless of what we do or how hard we try, we are unable to produce the desired results. Such was the case in Joe's life, as we saw at the beginning of this chapter.

Some adult children have told me they are simply stressed out, that the responsibility of life is overwhelming. But stress is different from burnout. We experience stress when outside forces press down on us. Stress is a normal part of life that can help us learn and grow. However, when stress is prolonged, uninterrupted, unexpected, and unmanageable, it can cause us significant problems. Handling stress effectively is critical to healthy living.

Excessive, continuous stress can cause burnout. Burnout isn't a clinical psychiatric or psychological disorder, but it shares similarities with depression, anxiety disorders, and mood disorders. Burnout is usually less severe, it doesn't usually last as long, and it is caused by situational stress rather than a chemical imbalance. Still, when we're in the throes of burnout, our world can seem frighteningly unmanageable.

Symptoms of Burnout

Do any of these symptoms describe your life?

depleted physical energy

emotional exhaustion

lowered immunity to illness

less investment in interpersonal relationships

increasingly pessimistic outlook

increased absenteeism and inefficiency at work

In most instances of burnout, the writing appeared on the wall long before it happened. Along the way, something told us something wasn't right, but we chose to continue the dance of dysfunction anyway.

Total burnout can take years to occur, and when it does, it is often the turning point in the life of an adult child. Such was the case in Joe's life. His world came crashing down on him, yet he was only trying to help.

Helping is good. Being there for your parents is good. And sacrifice is often necessary. But should you sacrifice your marriage, family, job, and self-respect? Should you sacrifice your emotional, physical, financial, mental, and spiritual health?

You can love and care for someone without losing yourself (and your sanity) in the process. You can help people and even sacrifice for them without significantly damaging yourself. As our parents grow older and require increased care and attention, we must learn how to help them without significantly hurting ourselves and others we love and are called to protect.

Please, don't get me wrong. Some pain in life is inevitable and even required as we grow. Sacrifice is sometimes necessary in our lives as maturing adult children. It may bring new meaning and stretch our capacity to love. God may call us to times of sacrifice and obedience. And some of those times will necessarily be painful. Yet even during times of sacrifice, God commands us to guard our hearts and protect our relationships as good stewards.

If you read the first *Setting Boundaries* book, you know that I'm a classic enabler. I thought for years that I was helping my son, but I was doing quite the opposite. I'll reiterate my definition of an enabler and the difference between helping and enabling. As you read, you may be able to determine whether enabling is part of your problem with your aging parent.

The Difference Between Helping and Enabling

We help others when we do things for them that they cannot do for themselves. We also help others by empowering them to stop their own detrimental behaviors.

On the other hand, we enable others when we do things for them that they can and should do themselves. We also enable them when

we recognize that they have recurring problems and
continue their detrimental behaviors. You enable y
when you create an atmosphere in which they can
tinue their unacceptable behavior.

For years I unknowingly handicapped my adult child by doing
things for him that he should have been doing for himself. I also contributed to the ongoing chaos, crisis, and drama in our relationship
by focusing on my son's problems and his poor choices. I was trying
to fix him and change him instead of looking at my part in our dysfunctional situation.

I created an environment in which he could comfortably continue
his unacceptable behavior. I didn't set healthy boundaries and consistently enforce them. Instead, I lived my life in an almost constant
state of stress trying to juggle it all and justify my motives. When I
burned out, not much was left but ashes.

We Can Change Our Responses

I knew the way my son was living was wrong and that his choices
were leading him on a path of destruction. But it took years to learn
that I'm responsible for only my own decisions, not his. I couldn't make
him change his life. I could, however, change my own. I could also
change my responses to his choices. I could learn to love him without
being responsible for him, and I could set clear boundaries in order to
live a life of passion and purpose that was pleasing to God.

"You don't understand, Allison. It's not the same. I feel responsible
for my parents. How can I sit back and watch them…"

Believe me, I hear what you're saying. Please look closely at your
situation to see if you're confusing responsibility with enabling. Are
you doing for your aging parents what they might be capable of doing
for themselves?

As time takes its toll, our aging parents may become increasingly
incapacitated and need us to take on more care and responsibility. Yet
this is a gray area. What can our parents do for themselves, and what
can they not do? What is our responsibility, and what is not? If you

struggling daily (sometimes hourly) to avoid burnout because you re trying to do it all, let the following simple truth open the door to hope and healing to your life.

A Simple Truth

Unless we are cognitively diminished and our parents have remained our legal guardians, the way we live our lives and our personal choices are up to us, not our parents. And unless our parents are cognitively diminished and we have become their legal guardians, the way they live their lives and their personal choices are up to them, not us—regardless of how old they are and how responsible we feel.

Living by this simple truth doesn't make us cold, uncaring, or selfish. It shows that we are mature enough to live our own lives while respecting our parents' right to do the same. Many adult children treat their aging parents like children. Is it any wonder some of our parents have begun to act the part? These adult children have overstepped their aging parents' boundaries. Our job is to love and honor our parents, not to live their lives for them or second-guess what we think or feel is best for them simply because they are getting older. That's not our job unless they are cognitively diminished and we are legally responsible.

Our aging parents may not be so cognitively diminished that we have to take full legal guardianship, but advanced age may nonetheless be taking its toll. We want to be there for them when their mental acuity and physical abilities waiver. This may include stepping in on occasion and accepting responsibility. Setting healthy boundaries is not a generic excuse to jettison our aging parents into a black hole where they must fend for themselves no matter what. Selfishness is never justified. That is not at all the purpose of healthy boundaries.

The goal of the Six Steps to SANITY is to help us guard our hearts, stay right with God, and gain wisdom to make rational choices in every area of our lives. We set healthy boundaries so we can truly benefit ourselves, our families, and our parents in authentic and loving ways.

We don't want to implement boundaries that will cause us regrets after our parents have left this earth. Death may eventually end a life, but it does not end a relationship. We want the memories from this season of life to be as loving and authentic as possible under whatever circumstances. We want to honestly say we did our best.

But this book focuses on situations and circumstances where you long for a better relationship with your parents but feel trapped in a seemingly never-ending cycle of chaos, crisis, or drama. Your parents are in control and are making very poor choices.

The dad who promised to make the car payments should have kept his promise. The mom whose rent was graciously being subsidized by her daughter and son-in-law should not have permitted her unemployed man-friend to move in with her. The parents who were allowing their son to supplement their income while they were giving financial support to their drug-addicted daughter clearly had their own enabling issues. These parents all had choices, and as adults, they need to remain accountable for those choices.

In my work with parents who want to stop enabling their chronically dependent adult children, I've seen that this critical area of accountability is one of the most difficult for them to change. The consequences of our adult children's choices can be quite severe, so we've tried for years to protect them from experiencing them.

Are we as adult children responsible to take on the consequences of our parents' actions? We may wonder whether our aging parents are responsible for the consequences of their choices. But their age, physical handicap, and financial status are not excuses for them to be irresponsible or disrespectful. Are we truly helping our aging parents—as countless generous caregivers around the world are doing—or are we contributing to their problems by enabling them to comfortably continue negative behavior?

And what about consequences that may occur as a direct result of new boundaries we might establish? When parents set firm boundaries with adult children, their primary goal is almost always the same—to cut the apron strings and launch the adult children into an independent lifestyle. But this isn't the case with our aging parents. Instead of going from dependence to independence, it's often the opposite.

We love our parents, and we want to do what is best and right for them. But in our zeal to do what we think is right, we may end up making poor choices. The road to setting boundaries with our parents is paved with a multitude of variables we must consider. The issues are seldom black-and-white.

In the seminal collection of essays addressing the caregiving journey, *Eldercare for the Christian Family*, editor Timothy S. Smick writes about one of those variables.

> Unlike parents of young children, who anticipate each step of early childhood development, adult children of senior parents must deal with an unpredictable calendar of physical aging. Some seniors have the capacity to live engaging and active lifestyles. At age 90 they are capable of running their own lives and sometimes try to dominate their children's too.[4]

Of the 305 million people in the United States, 79 million are baby boomers, born between 1946 and 1964. Many of these will find themselves caring for aging parents. You are likely one of them. Consider these statistics:

- In 2006, 37.3 million Americans were 65 or older. They represented 12.4 percent of our country's population—about one in every eight Americans. By 2030, about 71.5 million people will be 65 or older—more than 20 percent of the population, and more than twice their number in 2000.[5]

- In 2004, the National Alliance for Caregiving and AARP estimated that 61 percent of those who voluntarily cared for elderly people—usually their own relatives—were women. Among those women, 41 percent were working full-time jobs at the same time.[6]

- The number of centenarians in the United States grew from 15,000 in 1980 to 77,000 in 2000.

America is aging! And in addition to the unpredictable calendar of physical aging Timothy Smick shared, a myriad of other life circumstances are thrown into the mix. Some adult children I have talked to have parents who live independently. Other parents live with their children, or they are in assisted-living facilities, or they have full-time care at home. Some parents are widowed, others are celebrating many decades of marriage. Some parents are kind and loving, others are manipulative, bitter, and toxic. Some are open to experiencing new things in life, and others are stubborn as mules. Some adult children have parents in their forties and other parents are well into their nineties. But all of the adult children who struggled with their parents had this in common: They felt powerless, as though they had no options or choices in their difficult situations with their parents.

Actually, we have many choices, and my prayer is that I can help you recognize yours.

A Question of Honor

When I talk with adult children about their aging parents, they often mention honor and respect. In fact, setting boundaries with parents *requires* addressing the subject of honor. Scripture provides a clear mandate: "Honor your father and your mother, so that you may live long in the land the LORD your God is giving you" (Exodus 20:12).

But people's understanding of these words is often warped and confused. The question isn't whether we are to honor our parents. The answer to that is clear: Yes, we are. Rather, we must ask whether our actions are honoring or dishonoring them. When we establish healthy boundaries with our parents, boundaries that will stop their inappropriate behavior and prevent situations that cause pain for everyone involved, aren't we honoring them? Aren't we honoring them when we hold them accountable and speak the truth in love? Does simply telling our parents *no* imply that we are dishonoring them?

Many people struggle with the answers to these questions, and they wander in a dismal valley of confusion. Statistics show that heart attacks, depression, divorce, and stress-related illness in baby boomers are soaring. We are clearly facing burnout in record numbers, partly because we're

> Come to me, all you who
> are weary and burdened,
> and I will give you rest. Take
> my yoke upon you and learn
> from me, for I am gentle
> and humble in heart, and
> you will find rest for your
> souls. For my yoke is easy
> and my burden is light.
>
> MATTHEW 11:28-30

confused about helping and enabling, honor and disrespect, accountability and irresponsibility, love and fear. Countless adult children across America are struggling daily to find balance as they juggle responsibilities and strive valiantly to do it all.

Regardless of our age or circumstances, God does not want us to live with undue stress. He does not wish for us to burn out, to be unable to care for own well-being, let alone the well-being of others. His Word is clear.

Can We Avoid Burnout and Build Respect? How?

We need to believe that a better life is possible. We can stop feeling like gerbils spinning on the wheel of life and going nowhere fast. We can address and eliminate our overwhelming sense of guilt. We can stop beings martyrs, doormats, and control freaks. We can stop responding emotionally and learn to respond rationally. We can nurture truly loving and respectful relationships with our aging parents that honor them and God without losing ourselves in the process. We can get healthy and take back our lives. We can find sanity!

To do that, we need to start with two critical tasks:

1. We must understand how we got to this place of burnout.

2. We must understand how we get out.

Sounds pretty easy, right? In some ways it can be. I've received hundreds of e-mails and letters since releasing *Setting Boundaries with Your Adult Children* and launching the Six Steps to SANITY and 12 Weeks to Freedom programs. A common thread runs throughout many of these notes.

"I can't believe the freedom I felt...how the lightbulb went on..."

"SANITY was all I needed...I got my life back!"

"It was hard at first...but the peace we have now is priceless..."

To understand how we got here and how we can get out, we'll learn how to...

obey God

pray and reflect

establish priorities

respect ourselves

develop new skills and coping strategies

take off the blinders and look in the mirror

find SANITY

And as we've seen, you can find sanity if you...

S—Stop your own negative behavior.

A—Assemble a support group.

N—Nip excuses in the bud.

I—Implement rules and boundaries.

T—Trust your instincts.

Y—Yield everything to God.

To help us on the journey, "Balancing Actions" will appear at the end of every chapter, suggesting tasks you can accomplish to help you find balance and sanity. In summation, Cloud and Townsend add:

> The ultimate goal of learning boundaries is to free us up to protect, nurture, and develop the lives God has given us stewardship over. Setting boundaries is mature, proactive, initiative taking. It is being in control of our lives.

  Individuals with mature boundaries aren't frantic, in a hurry, or out of control. They have a direction in their life, a steady moving toward their personal goals. They plan ahead.[7]

That's what we're going to learn to do—to plan ahead as much as we are able. We're going to learn to set healthy boundaries so we can truly help ourselves, our families, and our aging parents in authentic and loving ways. We're going to become mature individuals by avoiding burnout and building mutual respect.

Balancing Actions

1. Buy a spiral notebook, journal, or something else you can use to begin keeping notes. Nothing fancy. No one will see this unless you choose to share it.

2. List some things you have learned so far about setting boundaries with your aging parents.

3. List some things you have learned so far about yourself.

1

The Road to Burnout

At 3:25 p.m. on January 15, 2009, US Airways Flight 1549 took off from New York's LaGuardia Airport. Moments later, it was struck by a flock of geese, causing its engines to fail. Captain Chesley "Sully" Sullenberger piloted one of the most remarkable emergency landings in aviation history, saving the lives of all 155 on board.

He later reflected on a discussion he had with his daughter, Kate, when she was nine years old.

> I was driving her to school one day, and out of the blue, she asked me, "Daddy, what does integrity mean?"
>
> After thinking about it, I came up with what, in retrospect, was a pretty good answer: "Integrity means doing the right thing even when it's not convenient."[1]

Being a Christ follower also includes doing plenty of things that aren't convenient or easy. God calls us to be people of integrity—to do the right things. And often, there's nothing convenient (or easy) about it. In fact, in a world where tolerance has been raised to an art form, knowing what the right thing is can be difficult.

Does the right thing include compromising the health and sanity of your own life and the life of your family as you care for your aging parents? That's a difficult question only you can answer. But if your answer is yes, what happens to your aging parents when you've gone past your breaking point? How does that help them?

It's true, we won't always have our parents. The time will come when God calls them home. How will you remember their last years—as a bitter battlefield of will and woe, or with loving memories for the season you experienced together? You build beautiful memories partly by setting healthy boundaries.

Adult children from all around the country tell me about their desire to walk in God's will as they relate to their aging parents. Yet we aren't always sure what this means. How responsible are we for them? Cloud and Townsend address this:

> Some people were born to take care of their parents. They did not sign up for this duty; they inherited it. Today we call these people "codependent." Early in life they learned they were responsible for their parents, who were stuck in childish patterns of irresponsibility. When they became adults, they had a difficult time setting boundaries between themselves and their irresponsible parents. Every time they tried to have separate lives, they felt selfish.
>
> Indeed, the Bible teaches that adult children should take care of their elderly parents. "Give proper recognition to those widows who are really in need. But if a widow has children or grandchildren, these should learn first of all to put their religion into practice by caring for their own family and so repaying their parents and grandparents, for this is pleasing to God" (1 Timothy 5:3-4). It is good to feel grateful to our parents and to repay them for what they have done for us.[2]

Yes, it's good to feel grateful. However, does being grateful also mean we must willingly accept negative, harmful, and cruel behavior from our aging parents? In the passage above, Paul teaches that proper recognition should be given to those who are really in need. How do we know when our aging parents are really in need? Cloud and Townsend have more to say about this particular situation.

But two problems generally crop up. First, your parents may not be "really in need." They may be irresponsible, demanding, or acting like martyrs. They may need to take responsibility for their own knapsacks.

Second, when they are "really in need," you may not have clear boundaries to determine what you can give and what you can't give. You may not be able to limit your giving, and your parents' inability to adjust to old age, for example, will dominate your family. Such domination can ruin marriages and hurt children. A family needs to decide what they want to give and what they do not want to give, so they will continue to love and appreciate the parent and not grow resentful.

Good boundaries prevent resentment. It is good to give. Make sure, however, that it is the proper amount for your situation and resources.[3]

What is the proper amount? Have your emotional, physical, and financial resources been stretched to the maximum, leaving you burned-out, resentful, and just plain angry? Have you reached a point in your life where enough is enough? How do you determine if your parents are really in need? And when is it your responsibility to help them?

One of the most damaging myths we've come to believe is that setting boundaries is selfish, that we should never say no to our parents. Cloud and Townsend devote an entire chapter to exploding the common misconceptions we've come to believe about setting boundaries. These few lines provide a good summary:

Don't boundaries turn us from other-centeredness to self-centeredness? The answer is no. Appropriate boundaries actually increase our ability to care about others. People with highly developed limits are the most caring people on earth.[4]

Being a caring person does not mean being an overly submissive doormat or an overly controlling steamroller. Either of these extremes will eventually lead to burnout.

Author and speaker Virelle Kidder knows firsthand about burnout and about caring for aging parents. In her empowering and inspirational book *Meet Me at the Well: Take a Month and Water Your Soul*, she shares her story.

> Two summers ago I walked into my doctor's office with hives. Actually I had chest pains too, and a jaw that was acting up. I was tired and feeling old. Just before I left the house, my wise husband, Steve, had said, "Tell Dr. Mastroianni I think you're depressed." I told the doctor adding a weak chuckle.
>
> "I knew it the minute you walked in the door." His gray mustache curled around a smile. "And it's about time!" he added.
>
> "What on earth do you mean?" I asked as he pumped up the blood pressure cuff.
>
> "Look at your life, Virelle," he said, and then listened quietly to the stethoscope for a moment. "Blood pressure's a little high too. Look at what you've been through the last few years. Did you think you were immune?" I guess I did.
>
> This much-loved doctor knew our family well. It's true; we've had a lot of "stuff" to deal with. I suppose it began many years earlier with a prodigal son (who's wonderful now, praise God!), then a child who struggled with regular bouts of mental illness, another daughter with lupus, a son with a heart problem, my own repeated surgeries, Steve's stressful job, financial challenges during and following the college years and five weddings, both our efforts at ministry, and now my mother's recent diagnosis with Alzheimer's and all that has accompanied it. I'd become so used to living with toxic levels of stress, I thought it was normal.[5]

Toxic levels of stress—can you relate? If not, could it be that you're in denial? Virelle was.

> I thought this was not supposed to happen to strong Christians. If we're in the Word every day and all prayed up, aren't we supposed to suck it up and go on forever? Yes, we often do, right to an early grave.

I heard a friend say once "Beauty may be skin deep, but stupid runs clear through." But stupid can seem so right, so spiritual, can't it? I only half listened to friends who cautioned me about overload, overwork, too much stress and responsibility. That is another name for pride.[6]

We know that pride goes before a fall—and burnout definitely qualifies as a fall! (The actual Scripture is Proverbs 16:18 and reads, "Prides goes before destruction, a haughty spirit before a fall.")

Many have said that the road to hell is paved with good intentions. If you are on the road to burnout, you must understand this:

Rest isn't laziness.

Boundaries aren't selfish.

Saying no isn't disrespectful.

Asking for help isn't weak.

You can begin now to make choices to change your course—to get off the road to burnout. If God has given you people to care for and love, He will see you through this season. But you're going to have to make some changes of your own.

My first book is called *God Allows U-Turns*. It's a compilation of true short stories by people from all walks of life, stories of second chances and new direction, stories of how it's never too late to change the course of our lives. Stories confirming that God not only *allows* U-turns but also continues to walk with us regardless of how many mistakes we make—regardless of how many times we have to turn around and change course.

We naturally want to make meaning of our lives. We were created in God's image, designed to live in a garden with everything we could ever want or need, yet we've lost sight of what that means.

In his book *Dealing with the CrazyMakers in Your Life*, David Hawkins recounts a story about the time he and his wife were at JFK Airport in New York, returning from a peaceful vacation. Having just spent two weeks in Spain at a resort town on the Mediterranean, the assault on their senses from the busy terminal was a wake-up call. "Our chaos detectors blared their alarm: too much, can't take it, sensory overload, and danger, get out now!"[7]

After taking time off, he and his wife were now attuned to the fact that what they were experiencing at the airport wasn't a rational way to live. The incessant din, the sardine-like cramming of bodies, people rushing and arguing, babies crying…it was too much at one time. This was not how God intended anyone to live.

Dr. Hawkins explains in more detail what we experience when we are dealing with crazy-making situations and personalities, and how we've come to accept this out-of-control life as something we cannot control. We've been living this way for so long that we don't understand how wrong this is. Many of us have broken chaos detectors. Our warning lights should be telling us that something is wrong, but they're not working.

We've spent years existing as human doings instead of as human beings. We are *doing* what is expected, doing things to gain acceptance, keep the peace, and earn points. Doing it all, often at the expense of *being* the people God created us to be. No wonder we don't really know who we are or what we want. No wonder we have so much trouble setting healthy boundaries.

I know what I don't *want,* you might be thinking. *I don't want to feel guilty, angry, used, controlled, or manipulated. I don't want to feel like I'm beginning to hate the people I love.*

Knowing what we don't want is good. Knowing how we got here and then doing something proactive to change the situation is even better.

How We Got Here

The problems in our relationships with our parents didn't happen all of a sudden because we took a wrong turn yesterday. We've made a series of wrong turns and wrong choices that have brought us here today. In her book *Parents, Teens and Boundaries: How to Draw the Line,* Jane Bluestein encourages us to reflect on this.

Few of us are especially adept at setting boundaries with anyone, and for good reason. Let's back up a bit.

When you were growing up, were you told that other people's needs were more important than yours? Were you rewarded for self-sacrificing and people-pleasing? Were you taught to obey and then shamed, hurt, or punished if you didn't? Were you chided for questioning authority? Were you taught to avoid conflict at any cost? Were you often told that you were responsible for someone else's feelings or behaviors? If you answer yes to most of these questions, the price was your sense of self, which is the foundation for boundary setting.

Was your privacy respected? Was it OK to have your own feelings and opinions? Were you encouraged to solve your own problems and supported through the process, or was someone always there to tell you what to do? Or did you spend just a little too much time fending for yourself, perhaps taking care of other family members with very little support? These experiences, too, influenced your sense of where you end and where others begin.

How do you typically respond to conflict? If your pattern is either one of rebellion or one of compliance, you probably haven't had much practice setting boundaries.

As a child, did you experience verbal, physical, emotional, or sexual abuse? It's hard to develop boundaries when any part of yourself, including your dignity and sense of worth, is violated.

Clearly, Boundary Setting 101 is not typically a part of a child's education. If anything, most of us have been conditioned to not set boundaries as a way to avoid the negative reactions of others. The ability to set boundaries to take care of yourself begins with the belief that your "self" is worth caring for. If we've learned that taking care of ourselves results in conflict, rejection, or abandonment, it's likely that we'll shut down when we need to set a boundary, rather than take that risk.[8]

I came across Dr. Bluestein's book doing research for *Setting*

Boundaries with Your Adult Children and found her insight to be especially helpful for the parents and grandparents I was addressing. They needed to identify their own parenting style to better understand how and why they were enabling their adult children.

Returning to her book with a new focus, I've found this a valuable resource in helping adult children better identify the parenting style of their aging parents. This is a key aspect to a better understanding of who we are.

> In addition, there has been, for most of us, a severe shortage of healthy role models. Most of the adults in our lives tend to fall into one of two categories: Bulldozers or Doormats.

> Bulldozers may appear to take care of themselves, but their version of self-care does not take other people's needs into consideration. Bulldozers need to win, to have their needs taken care of, and feel entitled to do so at the expense of the other person.

> This is not boundary-setting. Boundary-setting considers the needs of the other person, although it does not always accommodate them. In other words, "My way or the highway" is bulldozing, not boundary-setting.

> Doormats function as though they had no boundaries. They are agreeable, nice, FINE. (At least until their resentment builds up to one nasty tolerance break, after which they can make the meanest Bulldozer look pretty tame.) Doormats are terribly accommodating, but do so at the expense of their own needs. They tend to be on the losing end of most conflicts. However, by not sticking up for themselves, they not only avoid many conflicts, but they also get to "look good," be self-righteous, and validate a self-perception of helplessness and victimization. So when you think about it, there's a great payoff for being a Doormat, but there's also a high price to pay in the loss of one's self.

> Clearly, these patterns have nothing to do with boundary-setting, although Doormats often function in the hope that being "nice" enough will inspire the people around them to

figure out and accommodate their needs. Boundary-setting always takes one's own needs into account and relies on honest and direct communication (rather than manipulation and clairvoyance).

Growing up with either or both of these models, we receive a number of messages that present obstacles when we attempt to take care of ourselves in relationships with others, messages that connect our worth and lovability to our ability to please others. If most of the people in our lives operated on some form of win-lose method of conflict resolution, either by violating and disempowering (as a Bulldozer) or by self-abandoning (as a Doormat), it can be hard to imagine win-win solutions that consider the needs of all parties involved.[9]

Whew! That's a lot to take in, isn't it?

Dr. Bluestein's categories, Doormat and Bulldozer, appear to be universal parenting styles. Four distinct personality types are also universal.

To better understand how we got here, we need to look at many influences, including our own unique personalities and the role models we grew up with. We'll talk more about the dynamics of personality types in later chapters. In the meantime, let's talk about how we are supposed to be living.

As Dr. Bluestein wrote, "Boundary Setting 101 is not typically a part of a child's education." We also have little understanding of the concept and principles of setting boundaries God's way.

God's world is set up with laws and principles. Spiritual realities are as real as gravity, and if you do not know them, you will discover their effects. Just because we have not been taught these principles of life and relationships does not mean they will not rule. We need to know the principles God has woven into life and operate according to them.[10]

The Ten Laws of Boundaries

Many of us have broken what Cloud and Townsend call the laws of boundaries because we never learned them. We discuss many of these in coming chapters.

the law of sowing and reaping

the law of responsibility

the law of power

the law of respect

the law of motivation

the law of evaluation

the law of proactivity

the law of envy

the law of activity

the law of exposure[11]

If you realize things must change in your relationship with your aging parents and are ready to change direction, make new choices, fix your broken chaos detector, and apply the laws of boundaries, your first step toward sanity is to stop the insanity. That's where we'll start in the next chapter.

Balancing Actions

1. Today, take at least 15 minutes of quiet time alone to meditate, pray, and just think quietly.

2. What does the road to burnout look like in your life?

3. List the fears and concerns you have today regarding setting firm boundaries with your aging parents.

4. Lay these concerns before God and pray for wisdom to make godly choices as you embark on this journey of change.

Stop the Insanity!

Susan had waited until the end of my book signing to share her story. She had attended the women's retreat at the urging of her coworker.

"I don't belong to this church. I've never been to something like this." Her hand shook as she handed me her book.

"Did you enjoy it?" I signed her book, handing it back as I stood.

"Oh, yes, very much." She valiantly tried to blink back tears, and her voice cracked as she continued. "I didn't know about you or your book, but your talk was just what I needed. I just wanted to thank you for being so open, for telling it like it is."

I've heard heartrending stories of countless moms and dads as I travel the country speaking, so I've begun to pick up the silent signals of a parent in pain. Clearly this woman was teetering on the edge. "I'm in no hurry to go. Would you like talk?" I asked.

At that, the floodgates opened as she gave in to her emotions. I prepared myself to hear another story of a wayward adult child, praying silently for God to give me the right words to say should words be needed. Sometimes people just needed to be heard. Her words tumbled out like a rushing waterfall.

"We have three kids—all teenagers, but they're okay. I mean, they're all in high school, getting good grades. They're involved in sports and dance. They aren't the problem. It's my parents and my husband.

When you were talking about living a life of insanity, I could so relate. That's my life! It's crazy! My kids used to love being home, but now they hardly come home at all. They study with friends or stay late at school. My husband took another part-time job just to get out of the house. He used to be around to help me, but now I feel totally alone. I need sanity! We all do, but I don't know where to start."

We spent the next 45 minutes discussing her situation. About a year earlier, her father had a stroke that left him physically impaired but mentally sound. Her mother tried to care for him in their own home until the day she fell and broke her arm while helping him out of bed.

"Before she fell, Dad could get around with his walker, but he needed help to get in and out of bed and with meals and such, and all of a sudden Mom couldn't do it. Dad refused to go to a nursing home, even for a short time, and they couldn't afford full-time in-home care. We have a big house on acres of land, so we offered to let them live with us while they got back on their feet. I'm a stay-at-home mom, and the kids agreed to help. My husband was all for it at first. We leased my parents' house very quickly and put most of their things in storage and moved them in with us."

But things had not gone as planned. In fact, her father no longer used the walker and had stopped all physical therapy, preferring instead to use an electric wheelchair they purchased for him. His physical condition was declining daily as he refused to do any exercise whatsoever and expected others to attend to his needs. Her mother's arm had healed, although now she was dealing with a painful case of shingles. In their late seventies, they were mentally sharp but physically deteriorating.

"Last week Dad informed us that he wants to sell their house and add on to ours, to move in with us permanently. We have the land to do it and it makes sense to do it except...except..."

I encouraged her to just say it. "Except what? What are your concerns?"

She spoke so quickly I could barely keep up. This wasn't just a case of parents in physical decline. To make a long story short, Susan's parents were mean-spirited, negative, and verbally abusive. They argued with one another constantly, they didn't agree with her parenting choices, and they never hesitated to let her know. Their criticism and cruelty had totally alienated their grandchildren, and Susan felt as though she had become a prisoner in her own home.

Additionally, neither parent was a believer, and they belittled her and her husband for their faith. They mocked the Christian TV station Susan had on during the day as she worked around the house, so she had stopped watching it altogether.

"Game shows and shopping networks blare on the TV all day. It's driving me crazy!" I nodded and kept silent—no easy feat for me, but she needed to express her pain. "I'm not a nurse. I never wanted to be a nurse. I'm not good at it, and I miss my husband and my kids. I miss having them around, speaking with them. I know it's horrible to say, but I'm starting to hate my parents—and I hate myself for feeling this way. This isn't what I signed up for! What should I do?"

Another "What should I do?" question. In talking more with her, I learned that in addition to no longer watching programs on the Christian TV network, she hadn't opened her Bible in months, and her family never attended church anymore or shared quiet time together as a family. Red flags were flying high—this woman and her family needed help!

I greatly appreciate and respect the work Christian counselors and psychologists are doing around the country, so I informed her I was not a licensed counselor and encouraged her to locate a professional in her area. I assured her that seeking professional help was a courageous, proactive step, not something to feel guilty about. "But there is something you can do right now that might help," I said. What I was about to recommend wasn't a difficult step, but we often don't consider it because we're so entangled in the drama and crisis. Our chaos detectors are broken.

"I'll do whatever you tell me. I really am going crazy—I can't take much more of this."

I encouraged Susan to stop the insanity immediately by stepping back. She needed to temporarily remove herself from the situation, take time to be with God, and assess her priorities. I shared that often in our desire to help, we overlook a critical first step in making change.

"Susan, in order to change direction, we have to physically stop and turn around. If we feel like a gerbil on a wheel running at high speed but going nowhere, we need to stop running and get off. We need to make rational choices, and that's difficult to do when we're so emotionally involved."

One of our first priorities in stopping the insanity of any situation spinning out of control is to stop long enough to hear ourselves think. We'll talk more specifically about the Six Steps to SANITY in part 2, but to prepare your heart now to fully embrace the journey to sanity, you must stop, step back, and prioritize. You need a fresh perspective. You need to breathe. You need time with God.

Remember the five areas of boundaries we listed earlier?

> physical
>
> mental
>
> emotional
>
> financial
>
> spiritual

Boundaries define us. My boundaries define *what is me* and *what is not me*.[1]

Spiritual boundaries may appear last on this list, but they are by no means least. As followers of Christ, we must actively strive to keep our faith strong—to know spiritually *what is me* and *what is not me*. Unfortunately, when life gets overwhelming and our schedules get weighed down with responsibilities, our spiritual growth often suffers— our spiritual boundaries are violated. We talk to God in hasty prayers during times of stress, seldom taking time to be silent and listen to Him talk to us. In light of all that's on our plate, our quiet time with

God somehow seems selfish. Yet if we neglect to nurture a daily relationship with God, every area of our lives will begin to erode.

If you are in that place of quiet desperation—not knowing which step to take first—it's time to stop and go home to the place where Max Lucado says our hearts belong.

> God wants to be your dwelling place. He has no interest in being a weekend getaway or a Sunday bungalow or a summer cottage. Don't consider using God as a vacation cabin or an eventual retirement home. He wants you under his roof now and always. He wants to be your mailing address, your point of reference. He wants to be your home.
>
> For many this is a new thought. We think of God as a deity to discuss, not a place to dwell. We think of God as a mysterious miracle worker, not a house to live in. We think of God as a Creator to call on, not a home to reside in, but our Father wants to be much more. He wants to be the one in whom "we live and move and have our being" (Acts 17:28).[2]

The only way consistent growth in our faith can occur is through prayer, reflection, Bible study, and communication with the Lord. And the only way any of those things can take place is if we take the time to stop long enough to incorporate them into our day, every day.

"But I'm really not a very religious person, Allison," some have said to me as I travel the country and share this critical step.

"That's okay, neither am I," I respond.

You may have heard people say that Christianity isn't a religion; it's a relationship. That's what I'm talking about. My relationship with the Lord started late in my life—I was 35 and quite ensconced in the ways of the world. God has done (and continues to do) an amazing work of transformation in my life. But I'm a work in progress, as we all are. Nurturing this

> Seek first his kingdom and his righteousness, and all these things will be given to you as well.
>
> MATTHEW 6:33

relationship isn't always easy, but it's critical for my sanity. The same is true for you.

I can very easily get caught up in the insanity of living in the world and trying to juggle it all. I struggle with dyslexia and a serious case of AADD (adult attention deficit disorder). Either my brain doesn't consistently fire on all of its cylinders, or it's firing on all of them at the same time. This makes for daily challenges in many situations. Only when I consciously stop, step back, and remember the importance of spiritual priorities can I experience the peace that makes this crazy world not only bearable but understandable.

> Do not be anxious about anything, but in everything, by prayer and petition, with thanksgiving, present your requests to God. And the peace of God, which transcends all understanding, will guard your hearts and your minds in Christ Jesus.
>
> PHILIPPIANS 4:6-7

Of course, I had many concerns about Susan's situation. Hers was not a one-step-fixes-all scenario. Most situations with our aging parents are not. But we have to begin somewhere to find balance. We need to recharge our batteries and prioritize our lives.

Our aging parents are important to us, but our love for them and responsibility to them were never intended to be the altar at which we worship. I told Susan what I've been telling countless parents, grandparents, and now adult children for many months. "God must be at the center of our lives if we want to find sanity." In order to stop the insanity, we need to start nurturing a relationship with God, setting spiritual boundaries, and evaluating our priorities.

Nurturing a Relationship with God

As Christians, our first priority in life must be our relationship with the Lord. God is the head of our family, and He has established guidelines by which we are to live. To be obedient to God's Word and will is a lifelong calling. Listen to Cloud and Townsend:

When we become part of God's family, obeying his ways will sometimes cause conflict in our families and sometimes separate us (Matthew 10:35-37). Jesus says that our spiritual ties are the closest and most important (Matthew 12:46-50). Our true family is the family of God.

In this family, which is to be our strongest tie, things are done a certain way. We are to tell the truth, set limits, take and require responsibility, confront each other, forgive each other, and so on. Strong standards and values make this family run. And God will not allow it any other way in his family.[3]

As we take time to quiet our spirits and empty our hearts of the things that are not healthy, we must also take time to fill them back up with things that are. We need to spend time with God, not only talking but also listening. Kim Thomas in *Even God Rested* makes a valid point:

The silence that we may enter is not one of emptying ourselves out, but one of filling ourselves with the presence of this redeeming Christ. Silence is the time to drink deeply from his endless resources. It is a silence of body and mind, unto wholeness. Choosing silence or rest only when we are forced to by physical illness is the norm in our society. But that is not how we were designed. Silence breeds and incubates the goodness found in the remote places of our soul.[4]

Spiritual Priorities

We need quiet time to study the Bible and reflect on our place in God's kingdom. A powerful scriptural truth identifies our role as children of God. When we use this as the standard by which we live, it brings a level of peace to life that many of us lack. Cloud and Townsend write:

Numerous New Testament passages teach that we need to forsake our allegiance to our original family and become adopted by God (Matthew 23:9). God commands us to look

> to him as our father and have no parental intermediaries. Adults who are still holding an allegiance to earthly parents have not realized their new adoptive status.
>
> Many times we are not obeying the Word of God because we have not spiritually left home. We feel we still need to please our parents and their traditional ways of doing things rather than obey our new Father (Matthew 15:1-6).[5]

Please understand, this does not give us carte blanche to ignore our aging parents' needs. It is not justification to denigrate their position of honor as mandated by God. But it does give us a clearly defined boundary regarding allegiance, a standard by which we can live, learn, and mature.

Evaluating Our Priorities

We are a nation offtrack, off-kilter, off balance. Instead of worshipping God, we worship money, possessions, careers, youth, and worldly relationships. We see this in parents who have neglected to define their role, wanting instead to be best friends or pals to their children. We see this in parents and grandparents who consistently enable, fostering a generation of irresponsible, confused, and often addicted adult children. And we see this in the lives of adult children who have failed to mature in significant ways because of an inability to cut the cord that connects them to their parents. Examples of misplaced relationship priorities are all around us.

Yes, relationships are vital to life—especially our family relationships. Yet, as I said earlier, they were never intended to be the altar at which we worship. Scott and Sarah, two respondents to my questionnaire, learned the lesson of relationship priorities the hard way, as Scott shares:

> When my in-laws came to live with us, we weren't certain how long they had to live—they were both incredibly ill. For several years my wife and I put our lives basically on hold to care for them while working and trying to raise our own three

children. We never took a family vacation. In fact, we spent very little time together as a family, or even time for just the two of us to nurture our marriage. We were glad to be able to help, but it almost ruined us and our marriage. The time was stressful for everyone, and we missed so much in the lives of our kids. Those are years we'll never get back.

Thank God, my in-laws are doing better. They could be around for many more years—we hope they are—but we've come to realize that our children will only be young for this brief time. We want them to understand what it means to rise to the challenge of sacrificial love and to obey God. But we don't want them to look back on this time as a period that permanently damaged their hearts and souls or caused their parents to split up. We love Sarah's parents, but we needed to set a limit to our family's sacrifice. When we got our priorities in line, it was much easier to enforce the new boundaries we established. Actually, everyone is much happier.

Stopping and Starting

If we are in pain, we need to stop the cause of that pain—or change the way we think about the cause. But what exactly *is* the cause? Is the cause of Susan's pain the fact that her parents are mean-spirited and don't share her faith? Or could the cause have to do with her own priorities? Was Scott and Sarah's stress caused by her parents' failing health or by Scott and Sarah's confused priorities?

Whatever the case may be, this isn't the time to make hasty decisions, to set new boundaries based on emotions. You don't have to fix or resolve anything today. All you need to do right now is stop and step back. Temporarily disengage from whatever drama is consuming your life. Find time to be silent with God.

You must get a clearer picture of your reality. Remember, you are temporarily disengaging from stress, not running away (regardless of how much you may want to!). You'll have to return to face the situation, but when you do, you will bring your Spirit-controlled outlook and your desire to set healthy boundaries that honor God.

So don't simply disappear, leaving loved ones concerned about your health and safety. Inform them you are taking some time to be alone and reflect on your life and priorities. Take your Bible, a notebook to write in, this book, and anything else you may need.

If you are married, talk openly with your spouse and explain your need. Should you have underage and dependent children, make arrangements for their care. This isn't about running away from your responsibilities—it's about creating an opportunity to prioritize them properly. When you stop engaging in situations that cause stress and start spending time with God, you will begin to see the power of God in your life.

Be aware, however, that some of your family members may not be ready, willing, or able to embrace your new path. You may meet resistance, anger, fear, mistrust, abandonment, and other negative feelings. Do not let this sway your resolve to change. Remember, your ability to change is not predicated on anyone else's ability to change. This can be a very challenging aspect to setting healthy boundaries.

Balancing Actions

1. Read your Bible.

2. Now that you've stopped running, pray about the next step to take.

3. Visit a Christian bookstore and pick up a resource related to your need.

4. Write whatever God places on your heart.

It's All About Change and Choice

Many of our parents could benefit by changing and accepting the consequences of their choices. But the plain truth is that *we* must first accept the responsibility for our *own* choices—past, present, and future.

Our biggest issue isn't our parents' financial problems or what may become of them in the future if they don't make plans now. It isn't their gambling or alcohol addictions. It's not their old age, general stubbornness, or toxic behavior. It's not the mess we think they're making of their lives. Yes, these issues are important, and we have every right to be concerned about them. But when it comes to setting healthy boundaries, none of them are our biggest issue.

Our biggest issue is not any choice our parents make. Rather, our biggest issue is the way *we* respond to the choices they make. The biggest issue is *us*.

Ouch.

We need to realize that we are in control of our choices regardless of how we feel. And we need to make some changes. In his tiny but powerful book *Grace for the Moment*, Max Lucado offers great wisdom concerning change:

> God wants us to be just like Jesus.
>
> Isn't that good news? You aren't stuck with today's personality.

> You aren't condemned to "grumpydom." You are tweakable. Even if you've worried each day of your life, you needn't worry the rest of your life. So what if you were born a bigot? You don't have to die one.
>
> Where did we get the idea we can't change? From whence come statements such as, "It's just my nature to worry," or "I'll always be pessimistic. I'm just that way."...Who says? Would we make similar statements about our bodies? "It's just my nature to have a broken leg. I can't do anything about it." Of course not. If our bodies malfunction, we seek help. Shouldn't we do the same with our hearts? Shouldn't we seek aid for our sour attitudes? Can't we request treatment for our selfish tirades? Of course we can. Jesus can change our hearts. He wants us to have a heart like His.[1]

Where did we get the idea that we can't change? And why do we think our aging parents can't change? I can't tell you how many times I've heard an adult child say, "My parents will never change. It's an impossibility."

I don't know the details of your situation, but I do know this: Unless your parents have gone on to heaven, change is always possible. Sure, they may be stubborn. After years of repeatedly being fired in the oven of life, the baked-on crust of bad habits are hard to remove.

Hard, yes; impossible, no. With God, all things are possible.

Change can be a formidable enemy for some of our aging parents. It can pose challenges for us as well—often in unexpected ways.

Who Really Needs to Change?

"I've changed the style of my entire home several times over the past two decades," Rachel told me. "I love change. My parents, however, have the same furniture I grew up with. The only things they change are the clear plastic covers. It's like being in a time warp. The wallpaper in my old bedroom is still the same dusty pink cabbage rose print, for crying out loud!"

"And your point is?" I folded the dinner napkin, placed it on the table, and sat back, genuinely curious about her perception.

"Duh! The point is, Allison, they are living in the past. They're resistant to change, and I'm worried what's going to happen to them when the time comes to sell their place."

"Are they planning to sell?" I tore open a packet of sweetener to add to my hot herbal tea.

"Not yet, but they're in their eighties, for crying out loud. I can't imagine they'll be able to keep up with things for much longer." She pushed back her plate.

Says who? I thought. *Resistant to what change?* I wondered.

Carl and Louise, Rachel's parents, were two of the most vibrant people I had ever met. Sure, they were a bit eccentric, but hadn't they earned the right to be? Actually, I thought they were rather progressive. So what if they hadn't changed their furniture in years? They hadn't changed their car either, and it suited them just fine. Carl still drove a well-maintained, big, gas-guzzling black Lincoln Continental with suicide doors. (I had coveted that car for years and never missed the opportunity to tell him.)

The bottom line was that Rachel wanted them to change a certain way, and because they did not, she erroneously judged them as resistant and entrenched. In Rachel's mind, the problem was with them, not her. The fact is, many aging parents are doing just fine, thank you very much. The only thing many aging parents are lacking are adult children who respect them and their boundaries.

We're going to talk more about respect in a later chapter, but I've witnessed this particular scenario personally, and in talking with health-care professionals, I've learned that it seems to be more prevalent than we might think. Many adult children are selfishly imposing their own expectations on their parents, usually with horrible results.

We need to be realistic about how much our adult parents can comfortably change—or need to change, for that matter. Adult children often chastise their parents for being old-fashioned instead of embracing them and validating them for who they are. This makes for more than a little friction.

Change happened rapidly for us baby boomers. Some of us can recall early years without televisions, individual telephone lines, or modern appliances, and we watched with youthful fascination as a technological boom thrust us into the digital age. Advances came quickly with every new invention, and we welcomed them with open arms.

Many of our parents, however, do not share this same chameleon-like ability to rapidly adjust to change. They were raised in an entirely different era. Today's world is markedly different from the one in which our parents were raised. So here's the rub: We can probably embrace some aspects of change better than our parents can, but that doesn't give us the right to judge them or make them feel deficient.

What if we were to ask our adult children how well *we* adapt to change? How would they respond? Our adult children probably wish we would make some changes that we won't make simply because we don't want to. We aren't as different from our parents as we might think. Are you expecting your parents to make changes to suit you and your lifestyle? Are you willing to let them be comfortable and functional in their own way?

But What If They *Do* Need to Change?

Okay, let's say our aging parents really do need to change their attitude, behavior, or choices. Perhaps they *aren't* functioning well anymore. Or maybe something is really wrong, really toxic and harmful. Let's say they have a gambling problem, drink too much, criticize too much, or have decided to neglect their own well-being. Remember the simple truth I mentioned earlier? Unless our parents are cognitively diminished and we have become their legal guardians, they are responsible for their own lives and personal choices.

Our parents have the right to make their own choices regardless of whether we agree with them. You won't find sanity by convincing your parents to change. It's not about their choices. It's about *your responses* to their choices. *You* are the one who must change.

Perhaps you need to change by letting your parents make their own choices. Or maybe the time has come to make the difficult decision to step in and apply for legal guardianship of your parents. Declaring your parents' inability to make responsible decisions on their own behalf is a major step, but it might save their lives.

Perhaps your aging parents' cognitive ability isn't so compromised that you need to declare legal guardianship, but sometimes they are not acting in their best interest or in the best interest of others. Maybe they are driving when they can no longer see or react properly. Or they may no longer know their own physical limitations and accidently overextend themselves. In these instances, you must choose how to respond, knowing that your response may not be easy and that your parents may not welcome it. If you know something needs to change, take the next step. Make the commitment to change your choices before it's too late.

⌇

Three adult siblings lived in different states. They had been concerned for months about their father's declining health and the eventual need to sell his house. Their father was headstrong and had been unwilling to address the inevitable. So instead of meeting together in advance to develop a plan of action, the three adult children had done nothing. They had known some hard decisions were coming, but no one wanted to rock the boat or change the status quo by actually confronting their father with the truth, so they had silently chosen to do nothing.

But time ran out, and it was too late to process the situation effectively. Their father had worked all day in his yard in the hot Arizona sun, and he was hospitalized for malnutrition, dehydration, and a severe sunburn on the top of his bald head. "I was sure I wore my hat," he said to his oldest son, who arrived the next day.

The son had hastily arranged to take time from work, maxed out a credit card for various travel expenses, and rushed to his dad's side. His two other siblings were on their way and would arrive soon. This was the third time in one year they had come together for an emergency concerning their father.

Change Comes Down to Choice

Some things change with or without our involvement or consent. Unfortunately, most of those things are not likely to improve your relationship with your parents.

The positive changes that can improve your situation probably won't happen on their own. But here's the good news: You can initiate change! You always have a choice, and choice and change go hand in hand.

I have ongoing discussions about this topic with someone who is close to me. I tell her she has EE (extreme enabler) disorder. She replies that she doesn't enable; she simply does what she has to do. She has no choice.

"It's my responsibility, my obligation," she insists. "I have no choice."

I suggest that she does have a choice. In fact, she is making a choice. She *chooses* to feel obligated. That is her choice to make—I can't and don't want to tell her what to do, but I can help her see that she *is* making a choice.

Whether we are being responsible or irresponsible, loving and caring or angry and rude, our behaviors and responses to life's situations are not genetically programmed into our DNA. We *decide* to do what we do.

Some people feel powerless. They believe that they have no choice whatsoever in a matter, that things are happening to them over which they have no control. The truth is, feeling powerless is actually a choice. These people are surprised when they discover they have actually chosen to assume the role of those who have no choices—those who are powerless.

The freedom to choose is one of God's most precious gifts to us. But it's a gift that many people have not yet accepted. With an intellect and straightforward style I admire and respect, Dr. Laura Schlessinger has keen insight on this topic. She is a brilliant communicator with an uncanny ability to quickly assess a situation and cut right to the heart of an issue. She doesn't try to win any popularity contests, and her advice is often raw, but it's seldom wrong.

Dr. Laura devotes many of her books and radio time to people who make poor choices, people who are caught up in the bubble of insanity—repeating the same behavior and expecting different results. This is particularly common with people who have experienced early childhood traumas, as she explains in her book *Bad Childhood—Good Life*:

> While there has been a whole cottage industry dedicated to those who believe and identify themselves as injured or handi-capped by their childhoods—commonly known as victim, survivor, adult child of, or those with low self-esteem, or from a dysfunctional family—I believe that many people don't even realize that their childhood history has impacted their adult thought and behavioral patterns in unproductive ways. They don't realize that some of their less pleasant or destruc-tive adult emotional reactions are reflexive responses forged by their unfortunate childhood challenges. They don't realize that much of their adult life has been dedicated to repeating ugly childhood dynamics in an attempt to repair deep childhood hurts and longings. They are reduced to believing that neither they nor life matters much anyway, not understanding that they have the power and the choice to make a good life.[2]

Power to Choose

Could it be that your aging parents are *not* the cause of your con-fusion and pain? Could it be that your own choices have brought you to this place? And could it be that you have the power to change if only you will decide to? As I shared in *Setting Boundaries with Your Adult Children*, we cannot change others regardless of how much they may need to change. We can only be responsible for ourselves and the choices we make. This is not rocket science. It's good old-fashioned common sense.

Make Choices, Not Excuses

Sometimes instead of choosing to initiate change, we choose to make excuses. Excuses keep us in bondage by preventing us from resolving our relationship problems with our parents. Our excuses also enslave our aging parents by preventing them from becoming responsible for their actions and learning from the consequences.

"It's just so hard for seniors today."

"If I don't help, who will?"

"I'm only trying to help."

"No one understands my parents."

"They just need to find the right treatment program."

The excuses must end. We'll talk more about this in the N step in SANITY—nip excuses in the bud.

You may be thinking, *Allison, please don't make me feel even guiltier about my choices. I feel bad enough already.*

I totally understand. In fact, if you really want to get your life back, this attitude has to change too. It's time to stop feeling guilty. Take the spotlight off the situation with your parents and address your own burnout issue with proactive choices. Dr. Laura advocates making positive choices to regain the power that we have given away—regardless of what we may have experienced on the journey.

> While I suppose it is possible to sometimes make the case that a person was so traumatized and at such a vulnerable time in their lives that it became impossible for them to ever be happy or functional, I don't buy it. I do buy that it is a lot harder for some, due to their particular personality traits or magnitude of childhood problems, than others to take back their opportunities and potential. While I was in private practice, I saw people I thought were so damaged that perhaps they could not possibly pull a positive life together. I would sit, week after week, in awe of their grit and spirit in making the better (always scary) choices to improve their lives. Then there were the others who seemed to have so much going for them, with minimal external restraints, who almost seemed determined to not progress past the first chapter of their lives.

The obvious question is, "What makes some people hold on to being a victim and others choose to improve their lives?" The answer is control. When you are a perpetual victim, the past is in control of your present. When you are a conqueror, the present is controlled by your choices, in spite of the pain and the pull of your past.[3]

Changing Our Choices

Change won't always be easy. Some of us have been caught up in the dance of dysfunction for years. But it's never too late to change if we want to. We can choose to be conquerors. David Hawkins sums this up artfully:

> You and I must be able to make choices freely. Unfortunately, if you have been struggling with crazy-makers in your life, you may be addicted—in a loose sense of the word—to these people. You may be obsessively bound up in trying to change them instead of focusing your heart and soul on loving God, letting Him change you and give you wisdom for better ways of dealing with the situation.[4]

Why Change?

Many of us have known for quite some time that our insane situations need to change. We know our relationships with our aging parents are less than we hoped for. In fact, they often increase the stress in our lives and in the lives of those we love. We've been in pain for quite a while. However, we may not have considered that we are contributing to the problem by disobeying God's plan.

As we take time to better understand the road we've been traveling toward burnout, to stop, to step back, and to reflect on God's Word and His priorities for our lives, we can begin to look at specific ways we can change—ways we can choose different paths that will bring more balance to our lives.

Balancing Actions

1. In your journal, list your excuses for not changing.

2. Choose one thing to do today that will add balance to your life: spend time reading a good book, taking a walk, meet a friend for lunch, etc.

3. Spend time today with God; meditate on His characteristics and His love for you.

4

"I'm Only Trying to Help!"

Recognizing the difference between helping and enabling is a critical step in setting boundaries with anyone. Understanding what it means to be an enabler is equally crucial. Let's review the definition I shared earlier.

The Difference Between Helping and Enabling

We help others when we do things for them that they cannot do for themselves. We also help others by empowering them to stop their own detrimental behaviors.

On the other hand, we enable others when we do things for them that they can and should do themselves. We also enable them when we recognize that they have recurring problems and yet "help" them continue their detrimental behaviors. In other words, enabling creates an atmosphere in which others can comfortably continue their unacceptable behavior.

The caller we met at the beginning of this book—the one who complained about always loaning his dad money that was never repaid—is a perfect example. He knew his dad's behavior was wrong. He would never accept this kind of treatment from anyone else, like a sibling, friend, or coworker. Borrowing money and not repaying it is wrong. Yet by consistently loaning money that his dad never repaid, he created tuation in which his father could comfortably continue his actions. The caller was accepting unacceptable behavior!

Many adult children are not able to draw a line between their parents' acceptable and unacceptable behavior. We've somehow justified or excused behavior in our aging parents that we would never tolerate from anyone else. We treat them as if their status as parents makes them immune to doing what is right. This is not respect or honor. Some adult children live in a state of denial and are selectively oblivious to their parents' wrongdoing.

When we continue to accept our parents' unacceptable behaviors, we set a pattern with them that will be hard to change. We enable their repeated inappropriate behavior. Accepting what should be unacceptable behavior has become as natural as breathing for many of us.

Diane Viere, my partner in the Setting Boundaries outreach ministry and a certified Christian counselor, has discovered that many of her clients are not aware of the role they are playing. They are shocked to learn that they are enablers, as Diane shares in her response to my survey:

> Enabling is an insidious behavior. Although our desire is to help, when we don't set healthy boundaries around our helping, we begin to assume responsibility for every aspect of our aging parents' lives. It doesn't happen overtly, and we inadvertently generate a dependency. The more we do for them, the more dependent they become. The cycle of need and helping grows into a dependency that causes resentment for both parties involved: resentment from the caregiver, who becomes burdened, and eventual resentment from the care receiver, who begins to feel inadequate.
>
> Tensions increase, and silent hostilities roar. While they may not be evident at first, these conflicting emotions will eventually be revealed. When not directly and respectfully addressed, these conflicting emotions will burst out sideways—causing a cascade of disrespectful, inappropriate, and unacceptable behaviors.

Are you a bit fuzzy about what truly constitutes unacceptable behavior? Here's a short list that may help to sharpen your focus.

lying

violence and physical or emotional abuse

addictions

stealing

not making debt payments

manipulation by guilt

profanity

disrespectful behavior, especially around impressionable young children

Take a moment now and look at the list of 18 questions at the end of this chapter. They will help you determine whether you have been enabling your parents and sustaining the dysfunctional relationship.

By the way, I'm not saying we can never loan our parents cash or help them out financially. We just need to notice when asking for money becomes a habit. Parents are not entitled to the money their adult children earn, just as children (of any age) are not entitled to an endless flow of cash from their parents. A responsible adult repays a loan, but a habitual, irresponsible borrower seldom (if ever) repays it.

Dave Ramsey teaches in his Financial Peace program that if we are confident that helping out financially is the right thing to do and if we can afford it, we should *give* money to our family members in need and not loan it to them, thereby never experiencing problems if a loan cannot be repaid. This might limit our willingness to come to the rescue with cash, wouldn't you say?

As we consider a course of action, we should ask ourselves this key question: *Am I helping or enabling?* As difficult as it may be to admit, we may be somewhat responsible for the situation in which we find ourselves today. Some of us have surely played a part in the growing dysfunction of our family. We didn't know we were part of the problem. In fact, we thought we were helping. But now we know better.

✑

My mother loved crafting. She was always making things with yarn, beads, glitter paint, and fabric. Her collection of rubber stamps was amazing, and she used them to decorate greeting cards, bookmarks, and stationery. Now that she's gone, I'm so glad I saved every card she ever sent to me. The time she spent creating these love offerings made her feel vital, useful, connected, and engaged. I always felt special when I received them.

Often, when I visited her assisted-living home, we went to the craft room together or to the hair salon. (Shopping was more difficult because she wasn't very mobile.) I recall being in the craft room for a class, and we were making something using Popsicle sticks and beads. The sweetest woman sat next to my mom—I can't recall her name, but Mom knew her well. She was a resident on the same assisted-living floor, and like my mom, her challenges were more physical than emotional or mental. They were relatively good friends. Her daughter was also visiting and sat next to her.

As this precious elderly woman was stringing beads, I watched her get so excited about creating this little project—she was really having fun. At the same time, I watched her daughter get more and more agitated, clearly impatient with the slow progress her mother was making. Suddenly, she literally grabbed the project from her mother's hand and said, "Here, let me help you" as she proceeded to quickly string the beads.

The light went out of her mother's face. I watched sadly as her daughter robbed her joy and smothered her excitement. The daughter may have intended to be helpful, but her actions were actually cruel.

✑

Sometimes we adult children enable our aging parents, but that's not the only way we are contributing to our own burnout. Yes, we've encouraged negative behavior to continue by not setting appropriate and healthy boundaries, but sometimes we have also fostered weakness and resignation in our aging parents by treating them like little children. Sometimes we've been hurting our parents instead of helping them.

We have damaged their dignity.

Like the daughter who stepped in to complete her mother's project, we probably do this innocently, never intending to hurt or hinder. Yet we have. We have contributed to our parents' feelings of inadequacy. We enable our aging parents not only to continue negative behavior but also to give up, to retreat, to disengage from relationships and activities that help them feel wanted, needed, vital, and connected. In short, we foster weakness and resignation.

We have overstepped our parents' boundaries, and many of them don't realize what happened or don't know how to talk with us about it. They fear losing us as much as we fear losing them. Many adult children burn out because they try to live multiple lives—their own, their children's, and their aging parents'—all the while saying, "But I'm only trying to help!" We clearly need more wisdom and understanding. Hear Cloud and Townsend's wisdom:

> Made in the image of God, we were created to take responsibility for certain tasks. Part of taking responsibility, or ownership, is in knowing what is our job, and what isn't. Workers who continually take on duties that aren't theirs will eventually burn out. It takes wisdom to know what we should be doing and what we shouldn't. We can't do everything.[1]

Wisdom is not something we suddenly acquire, like fast food. "I'll take one order of wisdom to go, please." Wisdom comes from accumulated knowledge, insight, and judgment. It takes time to obtain. It also comes from God. "For the LORD gives wisdom, and from his mouth come knowledge and understanding" (Proverbs 2:6).

To understand the difference between helping and enabling, we need to clarify what is our responsibility and what is not. We also need to know the real meaning of honoring our parents.

Does Our Help Honor Them?

When we help our parents because we feel guilty, angry, or afraid, we aren't acting out of love for our parents. We aren't honoring them. We're doing something else entirely. Honoring your father and mother does not mean doing things for them that bring resentment, foster unacceptable behavior, or diminish their dignity. This is how Betty Benson Robertson explains honoring in her book *Changing Places:*

> The gratitude we feel toward our parents is sometimes tempered by resentment of the shortcomings and imperfections of their parenting style, whether perceived or actual. Honoring our parents however has nothing to do with whether or not we agree with the way they raised us or the way they've lived their lives. It doesn't even have to do with whether or not we like them. Honoring our parents entails rather not shaming them verbally or minimizing the investment they made in our lives.[2]

"Listen to your father, who gave you life, and do not despise your mother when she is old" (Proverbs 23:22). Yes, our parents gave us life, the ultimate investment. Yes, we are instructed to honor them as our parents. However, to honor them does not mean...

to enable them

to diminish their dignity

to accept abuse in any form

to excuse irresponsibility and disrespect

What motivates us to respond as we do? Why are we struggling with an inability to set healthy boundaries? We'll address these questions in the next chapter.

Balancing Actions

1. List some ways you have been reinforcing negative behaviors.

2. Write out the difference between helping and enabling.

3. Schedule some time to do an activity that you enjoy. Make it a high priority!

4. List some ways you have overstepped your aging parents' boundaries.

ARE YOU ENABLING YOUR PARENTS?

Here are a few questions that might help you determine the difference between helping and enabling your parents.

1. Have you repeatedly loaned your parents money without being repaid?

2. Have you made major purchases for your parents because you felt guilty?

3. Have you paid your parents' bills?

4. Have you accepted part of the blame for your parents' addictions or behavior?

5. Have you ever felt guilty for not being more _____ ? (Fill in the blank.)

6. Have you avoided talking about negative issues with your parents because you feared their response?

7. Have you bailed a parent out of jail or paid for legal fees?

8. Have you given a parent one more chance...and then another and another?

9. Have you wondered how your parents find money to buy cigarettes, play bingo, visit the casino, and such but can't afford to pay their own bills?

10. Have you begun to feel that you've reached the end of your rope with a parent?

11. Have you begun to resent your parents and yourself for the way you live?

12. Have you begun to worry that the financial burden is more than you can bear?

13. Have you begun to feel that your marriage is in jeopardy because of this situation?

14. Have you noticed other family members resenting your parents' influence?

15. Have you noticed that others are uncomfortable around you when this issue arises?

16. Have you noticed an increase in profanity, violence, or other unacceptable behavior?

17. Have you noticed that things are missing from your home, including money, valuables, and other personal property?

18. Are your instincts screaming that *something is very wrong*?

If you answered yes to several of these questions, chances are good that you have enabled your parents to avoid their responsibilities and escape the consequences of their actions. Rather than helping your parents to be responsible adults, you have helped them to get worse.

If you answered yes to most or all of these questions, you have not only been an enabler, you have probably become a major contributor to the growing and continuing problem.

It's time to stop.

5

The Motivation Behind the Madness

Changing your role in your family takes courage. The good news is that you can build up your courage to change by clarifying why you do what you do. The bad news, or perhaps just the challenging news, is that many of us have been so wrapped up in taking care of others—reacting to situations and propelling the gerbil's wheel—we've neglected to consider what may have fueled the fire of burnout in the first place.

How did we get here?

What makes us react as we do?

Who are we, apart from all this responsibility and guilt?

What motivates us?

By the time I began to seriously ask myself those questions, I was well into my third decade of life. Although many things were finally going right in my life, I had nonetheless developed some pretty unhealthy habits, and the worst had to do with the way I related to my adult son and his choices.

I loved my son and desired to help him, yet I was motivated a great deal of the time by fear and guilt. I was afraid of what would happen to him if I didn't come to his rescue, and I felt guilty for being a poor parent and role model when he was a child.

Motivated by Our Own Needs

Other motivating factors in my life had nothing whatsoever to do with my son. They were rooted in emotions and pain from my past—things I had never quite come to terms with. In many ways, my thinking was more than a bit off, especially concerning boundaries and balance. Dr. Laura addresses this in her book *Bad Childhood—Good Life*:

> Early coping and defensive strategies often become habits, and habits are behaviors that are reflexive, repetitive, and without much conscious thought. People generally do not recognize that their current behaviors were perhaps suited to their childhood circumstances, but not their immediate situations or relationships. That's why these behaviors and ways of thinking and interpreting events and others' intentions are unusually "off," not constructive, and annoying to others.[1]

You may be thinking, *Dredging up the past is so annoying. I don't have time for all of this childhood mumbo-jumbo. What's done is done—it's time to move on.* If that thought sounds familiar, I would like to ask you to reconsider.

What's done is *not* done, especially if your goal is to find balance in a life that is anything but balanced. You are never wasting time when you're learning more about who you are. If you're tempted to discount this chapter and the next, I would hazard to guess your closet might have a skeleton or two that you'd prefer to keep hidden.

Believe me, I know just how hard it can be to shine the light on your motives. Yet these exercises and emotional excursions are important. You need to be aware of how everything you have experienced is connected and makes you the person you are today.

Cloud and Townsend believe we often fail to set boundaries because we have false motives for doing what we do in the first place. We often give our time and energy (that is, we "help") for all the wrong reasons. Many of us parents are discovering we have enabled our adult children not because we love them or desire to help them, but because we are afraid of losing their love. That means our motives have almost nothing whatsoever to do with our adult children but rather are related to our own deep emotional triggers.

The reasons we do not set healthy boundaries with our parents are much the same. They often have more to do with our own emotional triggers than with what is truly best for our parents. Cloud and Townsend list some of the false motives that keep us from setting boundaries:

> fear of loss of love or abandonment
>
> fear of others' anger
>
> fear of loneliness
>
> fear of losing the "good me" inside
>
> guilt
>
> payback
>
> approval
>
> over-identification with others' losses[2]

A common school of thought widely accepted among professionals today is that our needs motivate our actions. Psychologist Abraham Maslow first introduced his concept of a hierarchy of needs in his 1943 paper "A Theory of Human Motivation" and his subsequent book *Motivation and Personality.* This hierarchy suggests that people are motivated to fulfill basic needs before moving on to other needs. It is most often displayed as a pyramid, with number one on the list (our most basic need) as the foundation of the pyramid.

1. physiological: breathing, food, water, and sleep
2. safety: security of body, employment, resources, morality, family, health, and property
3. love and belonging: friendship, family, and sexual intimacy
4. esteem: self-esteem, self-respect, confidence, achievement, respect of others, respect by others

5. self-actualization: morality, creativity, spontaneity, problem solving, lack of prejudice, acceptance of facts

We have five levels of needs. Shouldn't we strive to fulfill all of them?

Even with so much information available at our fingertips, many of us don't quite reach the top two tiers of the pyramid hierarchy—or if we do, we don't spend much time there because of the misconception that it's not the Christian thing to do. But seeking a better understanding of who we are by no means prevents us from trusting God and seeking His infinite plan for our lives. In fact, quite the opposite. And Maslow's hierarchy is not the only way to describe our needs. Here is another way to describe our motivating factors:

acceptance—the need for approval

independence—the need for individuality and
   competence

order—the need for organized, stable, predictable
   environments

physical activity—the need for exercise

power—the need for influence

social contact—the need for friends

status—the need to belong

tranquility—the need to be safe

Getting Help Is Good!

Many of us are hesitant not only to know ourselves better but also to seek help for what troubles us. As a certified Christian counselor, Diane Viere understands why reaching out for help is difficult for some.

> Too often, people in pain suffer in silence because they are
> afraid to expose their perceived ugly blemishes to a world
> that demands perfection. For Christians, the quandary of
> unanswered prayers, chronic pain, or sinful behavior remains

hidden in the recesses of our hearts because we fear judgment. So we hide, much like Adam "hid from God because [he] was naked" (Genesis 3:8-10)—it's our nature.

Yet God has gifted trained professionals with knowledge and wisdom to help His children to better understand the journey and be the best we can be. If we desire to better understand our own motivation and our family dynamics, we can begin by enlisting the aid of a professional. And should we ever find ourselves hanging on by a thread, this help can be lifesaving and life transforming.

Mark Sichel is a psychologist and the author of the book *Healing from Family Rifts: Ten Steps to Finding Peace After Being Cut Off from a Family Member.* He also graciously wrote the foreword to this book, and here addresses what can happen when we seek to better understand what motivates us.

> The unnerving news is that most of us have only very dim ideas of these family dynamics; few of us ever thought to question what gave rise to our own family's unique way of interacting. But there's good news, too: when you start to find out what makes your family tick—and explore your own complicity in keeping it ticking—you're on the way to a new liberation. You're en route to discovering you have a range of life-affirming choices in a realm that until now may have seemed like one in which you had few or none at all.[3]

Our Unique Personalities

Every personality type can have boundary issues. No one is immune.

Life experience adds color and texture to who we are, but every personality type has distinct traits. Remember the Bulldozer and Doormat descriptions? Those are two categories of parenting styles, but other systems of labeling personality styles are more popular, particularly the four basic temperaments that the Greek physician Hippocrates identified 400 years before Christ was born.

Before my first book was published, I attended a weekend workshop to learn about public speaking. It was led by Florence Littauer, the founder of Christian Leaders, Authors, and Speakers Services (CLASS) and the author of the bestselling book *Personality Plus*. In her book, Florence puts her own imprint on the four original temperaments. I already knew a little about the four temperaments before the workshop, but I learned a great deal more that weekend.

> We were all born with our own temperament traits, our raw material, our own kind of rock. Some of us are granite, some marble, some alabaster, some sandstone. Our type of rock doesn't change, but our shapes can be altered. So it is with our personalities. We start with our own set of inborn traits. Some of our qualities are beautiful with strains of gold. Some are blemished with fault lines of gray. Our circumstances, IQ, nationality, economics, environment, and parental influences can mold our personalities, but the rock underneath remains the same.[4]

Knowing the rock underneath, the raw material at the core of your personality, will help you understand yourself and know...

what you're made of

who you really are

why you react as you do

your strengths and how to amplify them

your weaknesses and how to overcome them[5]

The way Florence Littauer illustrated the strengths and weaknesses of every type was life changing for me.

The Four Temperaments

Hippocrates	Florence Littauer
Sanguine	Popular Sanguine
Choleric	Powerful Choleric
Phlegmatic	Peaceful Phlegmatic
Melancholy	Perfect Melancholy

Florence teaches two critical things about the temperaments that can change our lives:

1. We must examine our own strengths and weaknesses and learn how to accentuate our positives and eliminate our negatives.

2. We must understand other people and realize that they can be different from us without being wrong.[6]

> When we begin to understand the differences in our basic temperaments, it takes the pressure off our human relationships. We can look at each other's differences in a positive way and not try to make everyone be like us.[7]

How liberating! Just think, all those things your aging parents do to send you over the edge (and vice versa) may simply be the "raw material" underneath their personalities, and once you understand them better, you'll be able to communicate your boundaries in a way everyone can grasp.

If you are at all familiar with the four temperaments, you wouldn't need to be around me long to see I'm a Powerful Choleric—a dominant personality. We're known to be leaders, organizers, and communicators—goal-oriented, not necessarily relationship-oriented. This doesn't mean we don't need (or want) relationships, but the way we perceive and develop them is different from the way other personality types do. Remember, every temperament has both strengths and weaknesses.

This is important self-knowledge to possess, especially when we're looking at what motivates us to do the things we do. Why do we have boundary problems in the first place? Might our inborn temperaments predispose us to respond to others in certain ways? If so, what can we do to accentuate the positive and tone down the negative?

Unfortunately, when most of us were growing up, we were about as likely to learn about the temperaments as we were to learn about setting boundaries. We were not taught these things.

Of course, families are comprised of multiple temperaments—each person possesses strengths and weaknesses that make him or her unique. It's not always about being right or wrong. When families strive to understand and respect all the family members' unique temperament characteristics, they can enjoy a new harmony and be transformed.

Do you know your personality type? Your parents' types? Your strengths and weaknesses? Gaining insight into your personality and into the personality traits of others may be a good way to break the cycle of insanity. Remember the definition?

Insanity

Insanity is repeating the same behavior and expecting different results. Some families have been doing this for generations.

A host of psychological terms are associated with why we do the things we do—what motivates us. One of those terms was coined by Sigmund Freud—*repetition compulsion*. Of course, we are far more than a host of labels and jargon, yet in my experience of talking with countless parents and grandparents about the adult-child enabling epidemic, I have found repetition compulsion to be alive, well, and thriving! Sichel adds:

> This brings us to what Freud called "repetition compulsion," the compulsion to repeat behaviors and reenact family dramas in the unconscious hope that we'll resolve the dilemmas that gave rise to the need to repeat them. The trap is, when you're in the grip of a repetition compulsion, you only know you're doing "what feels right." But…"what feels right" sometimes turns out to be very wrong.[8]

Don't we know that! How many times have your best intentions backfired? Could those intentions have been rooted in false motives? Listen to Cloud and Townsend:

> The point is this: we were called into freedom, and this freedom results in gratitude, an overflowing heart, and love for others. To give bountifully has great reward. It is truly more blessed to give than to receive. If your giving is not leading to cheer, then you need to examine the Law of Motivation.

The Law of Motivation says this: Freedom first, service second. If you serve to get free of your fear, you are doomed to failure. Let God work on your fears, resolve them, and create some healthy boundaries to guard the freedom you were called to.[9]

Are we giving to our parents out of authentic love, compassion, honesty, and respect, or from a place of guilt, fear, resentment, anger, and bondage? Discovering what motivates us can free us from the bondage of poor choices. In the next chapter, we'll consider some things from the past that may be motivating us.

Balancing Actions

1. Discover your personality trait and learn about your strengths and weaknesses.

2. What motivates you the majority of the time?

3. What false motives have influenced you?

4. Do one thing to show love to your aging parents without responding to a need.

5. Take time today to quietly reflect on the blessings in your life.

Pain from the Past

In chapter 5, we saw that understanding our motivation can help us avoid burnout and build mutual respect. In this chapter we'll look at another critical step: We need to come to peace with our past and not be bogged down by it. We don't need to dwell forever on the trials and tribulations we have experienced, but we move forward by understanding the part they have played in making us who we are today. As Dr. Laura says, "Many people fail to understand the ways their histories impact their adult lives." Ray Pritchard agrees:

> Every year in January we talk about turning over a new leaf. For many people that means taking all of the leaves from last year and raking them over into this year. We don't turn anything over, we're just carrying our burdens and hurts from one year to the next; haunting memories, injured feelings and thoughts about the past that we can't get out of our minds. Some people live for years under the terrible burden of pain from the past. At some point we need to let go.[1]

However, this kind of self-awareness and personal growth can sometimes be painful. In many instances, we are dealing with highly sensitive topics, such as these:

trust issues

emotional scar tissue

wounds

suffering

the value of the relationship with your parents

I wrote the first *Setting Boundaries* book as I was learning the part I played in enabling my son, both in his youth and in his adult years. I really tried to be a good parent, yet I failed in many ways. The baggage I brought to my life as a parent was considerable. I had more than just emotional baggage; I had a truckload of dysfunctions. For a long time, I had to literally force myself in directions I knew were healthy and resist the negative pull to maintain the less painful status quo.

If we desire to change, we must identify our own issues—the things in our lives that keep us from being all God intends for us to be. Yet identification is not enough. We must do the work needed to heal from damage that may have occurred years or even decades earlier.

Coming to terms with pain from our past, learning to set healthy boundaries, consistently following up with the necessary and appropriate consequences…these things are not easy. Robertson in *Changing Places* mentions a situation:

> Beth successfully concealed her animosity for herself and her mother until her mother came to live with her. Then unpleasant childhood memories began to surface.

> Unresolved anger, bitterness and resentment are sometimes revealed in a negative reaction when the subject of caring for parents is broached. Painful memories from a past relationship can govern present feelings.[2]

For some, the road from burnout to respect is a rocky one.

"I'm 60 years old, for crying out loud," Carla said, wiping the tears from her eyes. "What happened to me as a kid in grade school is water under the bridge. It has nothing whatsoever to do with what's going on in my life now. Let's just move on to another subject, okay?"

Some of us shifted uncomfortably in our seats as the leader of our drama-therapy support group refused to move on and gently led this woman to a personal epiphany that moved us all to tears. I would hazard to guess that the event changed Carla's life forever.

The story has many facets, but the bottom line of her breakthrough was the realization that what had happened to her as a kid in grade school was precisely the reason she had spent years trying to get validation from other people. This pattern had caused her to be deeply dependent on other people to fill her needs—at any cost.

Carla had joined the support group because her husband had filed for divorce, both of her adult children were serving time in prison, and although her widowed mother lived in an assisted-living facility, the demands she made on Carla's life were oppressive. She said she felt like a doormat, and her life seemed to be coming apart at the seams.

It was a sad story. As a young girl, she had been raped on a school playground, and her parents swept the subject under a carpet, never to be discussed again. They moved on, but she had never been able to. For decades, she had looked to others to fulfill the emptiness in her life.

As she processed this decades-old memory in a therapeutic setting, she looked as if a huge weight were being lifted off her shoulders. I would like to think she went on to live a more fulfilling life—perhaps not immediately free of pain and worry, but surely with more hope and wisdom.

Why do we have boundary issues? Why are our relationships with our moms so strained? Why do we allow our dads to push our buttons time and time again? Sometimes in order to move forward we must first look back.

It took me years to slog through the muck and mire of my own issues, including a one-month stay in the New Life Clinic in Southern California in my thirties. Learning to change and grow required a concerted effort on my part. I'm thankful for several godly men and women whose professional training empowered me to unlock doors I needed to walk through. Their biblical wisdom helped me to understand the power of prayer and learn the true meaning of being a daughter of the King and having a living relationship with Jesus.

Schlessinger shares:

> I don't believe anyone does life well alone; I believe you lose your humanity by isolating yourself. This might mean you have to start with AA, psychotherapy or a prayer group. It's up to you to reach out. The intent of *Bad Childhood—Good Life* is to help you accept the truth of the assault on your psyche, understand your unique coping style and how it impacts your daily thoughts and actions and guide you into a life of more peace and happiness.[3]

If you find yourself stuck in an uncomfortable place, unsure of how to think or feel about a situation in your past, I encourage you to seek a reputable Christian psychologist or counselor in your area. It could transform your life.

Don't Get Stuck

A word of caution, however, as you delve into your history and motivations. This is a means to an end—not an excuse to remain frozen in time. Life is far too short to spend it living in the past. As I said earlier, sometimes to move forward you must first go back. But that doesn't give you carte blanche to throw yourself an extended pity party, make yourself the guest of honor, and invite everyone you have ever known to attend with you for perpetuity.

Get in, do the work, and get out. Do not become a victim. Remember, our goal is to avoid burnout and build mutual respect. But don't ignore the process either. Many of us have to deal with our past before we can set healthy boundaries in the present.

Our Parents Have a Past

For years I had a newspaper cartoon on my bulletin board. In it, a man sat alone in a very big auditorium. A banner on the front of the stage read, "Adult Children of Functional Families Annual Conference."

In other words, Ozzie and Harriet Nelson and Ward and June Cleaver may have been popular 50 years ago, but they were not the norm in real life. In fact, many of our parents came from families who had difficulty communicating, and their own tangled roots of pain and confusion may have caused them to inadvertently strangle something inside us when we were young. Who they are and what they have become could very well be results of emotional baggage they have carried around for many years.

If you think this might be hampering your parents' ability to cope, ask God to show you how you can truly help. Should you have a heart-to-heart talk with them? Suggest they meet with a Christian counselor or pastor? Is another family member better suited to approach them concerning sensitive topics? Perhaps helping your own parents come to grips with pain from their own past will help you process your own. But remember, your goal is to change yourself, not to change your parents. You have willingly embarked on this journey to set boundaries and find sanity, and the trip may necessitate dredging up a host of uncomfortable (or even painful or traumatic) emotions.

However, please be ultrasensitive to a critical fact: This may not be a trip your aging parents need or want to take with you. Move forward prayerfully in all areas and most especially in this one.

When reviewing your past, consider not only the context in which you lived it but also what you wish to achieve now by remembering it. Will sharing anything negative about your past with your aging parents now serve any fruitful purpose? Will discussing any harm they may have caused benefit anyone? Only you can answer that.

In most cases, the damage inflicted by our parents was not deliberate. Yet for some of us, the choking-off of our childhood was intentional—or of no concern at all. The evil in the world can take up residence even in Mommy and Daddy, and their toxic behaviors can continue throughout their lives, as we'll see in the next chapter.

Balancing Actions

1. Has this chapter called any painful memories to mind?

2. What have you learned over the years about how your past affects your present?

3. Write a letter to your parents about something in your past that weighs heavily on your heart. Do not deliver it. Put it away and read it again in a few days and then destroy it.

7

Toxic Elders and Destructive Choices

A dear friend of mine becomes a wreck every time her elderly mom comes for one of her indefinite visits. She spends weeks bracing herself for the onslaught of criticism. No matter how she tries, the hard hits invariably come, and she is left battered and bruised in the wake of her "loved one's" attention. It is mind-boggling how someone normally outgoing and confident can become a silent shell. I wish she could realize how the situation would change if boundaries were set. I would want her, as long as her mom is so inconsiderate of her, to stop allowing the visits in her home—her personal sanctuary—and instead set a different place (pay for it all if she has to in order to have the control), outline the days, and then leave when the time is up to continue on to other plans with her husband or daughters or friends. Her mom deciding the time, place, and length of the visit, along with her snarky attitudes, doesn't make for the right sort of captivating visit. Instead, the visit tends to end after a seeming hostage situation—including long stand-offs, negotiations, demands, and collateral damage.

Collateral damage indeed.

The story above was included in a response to this question on our questionnaire: "Do you know an adult child whose life is being torn

97

inside out by the actions, behavior, or choices his or her parent is making? If so, please share the situation and your opinion."

The mother in the story is a toxic elder, and the daughter needs to stop the insanity by setting some new boundaries.

Remember the cartoon I mentioned with the man sitting alone in the auditorium, waiting for the Adult Children of Functional Families annual conference to begin? I'd like to think there are more functional families in the world than that, but in case you're wondering what one looks like, here's a general overview.

Functional Families

Some families work hard to create an atmosphere of mutual support, love, and caring. They treat one another with warm emotional generosity. Members in a functional family are mature—they can control their emotions and communicate their feelings without judgment. They are accountable for their actions, they accept responsibility for their choices, and they refuse to avoid the consequences of their decisions.

Dysfunctional Families

Other families seem to breed or thrive on acrimony and dissonance. Anger, jealousy, resentment, bitterness, and sarcasm are a way of life. Members of dysfunctional families are governed by out-of-control emotions and unreasonable expectations, and many tend to be stuck in childlike behaviors. They tend to be irresponsible and to blame others for their lot in life.

Toxic elders typically live in dysfunctional families. These are the families where toxic parents may be a multigenerational influence that someone needs to break. Perhaps that someone is you.

What Is a Toxic Elder?

Toxic material is poisonous. It is harsh and can be malicious, debilitating, and even deadly. When parents become stubborn to a fault, excessively angry, belligerent, violent, or rude, they are toxic. When they make decisions and choices that are detrimental not only to their own health but also to your health and the health of your family and finances, they are toxic. When they consistently damage your spirit with their words or deeds, they are toxic.

To expose ourselves and our dependent and impressionable children to anything toxic would be unconscionable.

Sometimes, respect means saying no, but toxic elders don't typically get the *no* in *no*. And some of us with toxic parents have never properly learned how to say no. Maintaining a relationship with toxic elders requires tough love, persistence, and creative behavior modification. Sometimes, it requires separating entirely from them, a painful disconnect that is usually the result of much heartache and hurt.

People who responded to my survey question about toxic elders were quick to share an age-old adage: We can love the sinner and not the sin. Wendy Hamilton added this:

> Our parents are often not the people we would choose for them to be. Their choices and behaviors often do not reflect our dreams, our wishes and our goals. But we should still honor them by validating the unique people they are. We do not have to agree with who they are or what they do in order to appreciate all that God has done for them and for us through them. By allowing ourselves the distant full-screen view of our lives, we can see more of how God loves us. He is the parent with our best interests at heart. He is the parent who never fails us, never leaves us, and never forsakes us. When we agree with Him that our parents have value, our hearts soften and our thoughts about our aging parents change. By loving and respecting God more than our parents, we are able to love and respect parents who by all accounts and worldly standards are unlovable or unworthy of our respect. We love them at the place that God loves them—while they are imperfect and unworthy.

Learning to love this way is easier if we fully realize that God is our Father and He has adopted us as His beloved children.

> Do not call anyone on earth "father," for you have one Father, and he is in heaven.
>
> MATTHEW 23:9

Even if we have been in relationships with toxic elders for years, we are seldom prepared to respond rationally when adults (especially parents) disrespect us or hurt us. We do our best to turn the other cheek, often out of dutiful honor and respect, when we actually feel angry, resentful, and hurt.

Do any of these words describe your parents?

judgmental	sarcastic and rude	untrustworthy
critical	abusive	manipulative
condescending	mean and nasty	aggressive

If you answered yes to one or more of those words, you may have a toxic parent. But to think of a parent as poisonous is difficult and often painful. So, instead of living in reality, we often live in a make-believe land of wanting, wishing, needing, and even praying for things to be different. We continue like this for year after painful year, allowing the poison to slowly eat away at our self-respect. Often (as I've said before) we do this under the guise of honoring our parents. But we are called to honor their role as our parents—not their toxic behavior toward us.

If you have toxic parents and want to stop the insanity, begin by taking off the rose-colored glasses and seeing your loved ones as they really are, not as you wish they were.

One of the most helpful resources I can recommend to anyone having difficulty setting boundaries with toxic elders is the book I mentioned earlier by David Hawkins, a fellow Harvest House author. The first time I read *Dealing with the CrazyMakers in Your Life,* I did so for strictly personal reasons. I had been married to a crazymaker, and I was desperately trying to make sense of an unexpected and undesired divorce.

Dr. Hawkins has more than 35 years of counseling experience, and his book helped me turn a corner in my healing process—but in an unexpected way. Although I was able to clearly identify the crazy-making behavioral traits of my ex-husband (which I needed to do in order to understand how things had gone so wrong), I was also able to identify something far more helpful: the part my own crazy-making traits played in the erosion of our marriage.

When people we love are behaving badly, seeing the role we play is sometimes difficult. We get caught up in their poor choices, trying to make them change. They very well may need to change, but that's not the point.

The point is, we can control only the course we are on now, and if emotional pain is contributing to stress and burnout, it's time to stop and change direction. It's also time for many of us to switch our allegiance from earthly parents and become fully adopted by God—to stop allowing toxic elders to hurt us and to give God the rightful place of focus in our lives.

Let's face it. Some people are just plain mean-spirited. Some go beyond that and are manipulative, argumentative, stubborn, aggressive, abusive…in short, toxic. When you are around them, your joy is extinguished as the emotional air is sucked from the room. Some of these people may be our aging parents, and until God does a major overhaul of their hearts, spirits, and souls, very little we can do or say will change them.

Yet when we decide to make changes in the way we respond to toxic elders, things will change. The fear that a parent may respond unfavorably is real, although the outcome could surprise you. The example below is from Mark Sichel's book *Healing from Family Rifts*.

> Krista and Anthony, a recently married young couple who came to me for counseling as a result of Krista's exasperations with Anthony's mother, offer a telling example. Krista complained to me in a couple-counseling session with Anthony: "From the moment we married, Anthony's mother has attacked me—for my housekeeping, for not giving Anthony the right food, for paying too much attention to my job, spending too much money—the list goes on. At first I just put up with it,

but now it's gotten to the point where I've decided I just won't speak to her anymore. That's it—I've had enough. I won't even take a phone call from the woman. Anthony may have to put up with her, but I'm not used to this kind of abuse, and I'm just not going to take it."

Anthony was miserable about the standoff. He knew there was a good deal of truth to what Krista was saying, but he was between a long-familiar rock and a hard place. "Look," he said. "She's my mother. I've always had to deal with her criticism, to put up with this. I know it's hard, but it's just how it is. I don't know why Krista can't learn to tough this out and not let it bother her so much. I mean, when you get married, you get the whole family package. If I could change my mother, I would. But I can't."[1]

This is a classic example of change and choice. It's not about Anthony changing his mother. It's about Anthony changing the way he responds to her. It's about looking inward at what makes him tick—his motivations, his past—and learning why he has been tolerating this kind of ongoing toxic abuse from his mother.

And it's about looking outward, at the bigger picture, the spiritual picture, and obeying God's command as Father. It's about Anthony stopping the insanity long enough to step back and look at his priority—his wife—and doing the right thing.

Scripture reveals the standard for our relationship with our parents. It began in the Garden of Eden when God created Eve for Adam to love: "For this reason a man will leave his father and mother and be united to his wife, and they will become one flesh" (Genesis 2:24). Let's see how Anthony and Krista handled things.

Krista wasn't the only one refusing to communicate with Anthony's mother. He didn't realize that he'd refused to communicate with his mother as well. Because he was so afraid to provoke her, his only mode was to placate her. It wasn't until Anthony began to realize that his mother's expectations were part of a family drama in which *he* had also taken part—that his subservience to his mother meant he had as much complicity in keeping this drama of abuse going as his mother did—that he began to be able to step out of that drama and heal from its toxic effects. Doing this not only ultimately enabled him to relate to his mother more openly—to stop shutting down and start communicating honestly with her—but helped him to communicate better with Krista as well.[2]

Fortunately for this young couple, they were able to work through this challenge early in their marriage. Anthony made the choice to change—to be obedient to God's standard by placing his wife in right priority. Alas, for many, the bad habits of enabling choices have continued for years. Long-established patterns of negative behavior are difficult to change, whether they are our own or our aging parents.

Difficult, but not impossible. Never underestimate God's power to perform miracles when we realize our complicity in toxic relationships, identify where boundaries have been scarce, and begin to do the work needed to change.

If your situation includes toxic elders, you'll have some hard decisions to make, especially if these parents are living with you. Poison can infect everything it touches—and your priority is to guard your heart, love your spouse, and protect your children.

Some toxic elders will never change. Will we continue to be held prisoner by their behavior, or will we do what we can to change the part we play in the drama? Will we break the cycle and model new behavior for our children? Ending a relationship with a toxic parent is seldom easy, yet it might be the most positive thing you can do for yourself and for your family.

Whatever decisions you make, remember the goal: to act out of authentic love, to respond with rational thought and control, and to avoid reacting emotionally. Remember to stop, step back, and prioritize. Ask God to give you supernatural wisdom and strength to do the right thing.

Clearly, not all challenging aging parents are toxic. Some may be as confused as we are about expressing what they feel in constructive ways, and their frustration causes them to respond emotionally and at times irrationally. Whatever your case may be, God is doing a mighty work in His kingdom to repair broken families. I've witnessed the healing of hundreds of people as they make conscious choices to change their thoughts and enabling behaviors with their family members. In the course of those miraculous transformations, some of those other family members are also making their way back to right thinking and right living.

My adult son is an example of this as he walks his own Damascus road every day—a road that increases his faith and wisdom and brings him closer to God, and us closer as mother and son. This road has us on an extraordinary journey of relationship restoration—something I've long prayed for. This will be our "What happens after the boundaries are set?" moment. As you strive to set boundaries and avoid burnout with your aging parents, never underestimate what God will do in your life, your family's life, and perhaps in the life of your aging parent as well. Our Father God is the author of love and forgiveness, and He wants what is best for us and for our parents. We'll explore some exciting possibilities about that in the next chapter.

Balancing Actions

1. If you have toxic parents, list ways you can set healthy boundaries to guard your heart.

2. How would Jesus respond to your toxic parents if He were to meet them today?

3. What would the consequences be if you made the decision to temporarily distance yourself physically and emotionally from your toxic parent?

8

The Power of Love and Forgiveness

Our love, honor, and respect for our aging parents shouldn't be contingent on their ability to love, honor, and respect us. This is one of the most difficult truths for followers of Christ to accept. And it often gets us hung up when we confuse love, honor, and respect with acceptance of negative (and perhaps toxic) behaviors that hurt us and our families.

When we can set healthy boundaries while simultaneously expressing love, honor, and respect, we are being obedient to God.

Years ago as a very new believer, a woman in my Bible study introduced me to a local Christian bookstore, and I was hooked. I had no idea there were so many faith-based books! It was the spring of 1989, and books written by Christian authors with decidedly Christian themes were not as widely distributed as they are today.

I was hungry to learn, so I purchased a great many books that day. But the one I remember the most (and that I still have on my bookshelf today) was a memoir by a young woman whose story had a profound impact on my life, especially in relation to my ability to forgive my mother.

Our personal stories were somewhat similar (at least our poor choices were), although the experiences with our mothers were quite the opposite. My mother had not been at all abusive to me, yet the pain I felt from her inability to express love and the denial she exhibited for years about the childhood trauma she knew I had experienced had left deep scars on my heart. I struggled to forgive her. And not only her—I was stuck on the whole issue of forgiveness in general. I could not seem to wrap my brain around forgiving those who had hurt me.

Yet Stormie Omartian had managed to do just that and more. She had managed, with God's help, to forgive under the most extreme situations. As I read *Stormie*, I began to understand how God can work to restore, redeem, and even renovate broken hearts and souls.

> The most important thing to remember when it comes to forgiving is that forgiveness doesn't make the other person right, it makes you free. The best way to turn anger, bitterness, hatred, and resentment for someone into love is to pray for that person. God softens your heart when you do and brings wholeness into your life.[1]

Loving our aging parents can be disappointing if our motives are wrong. Yet loving with clearly defined boundaries can powerfully change our relationships.

I asked this in the questionnaire I distributed: "When parents make harmful and negative choices that directly affect their adult children (or their families), should the adult children turn the other cheek and maintain harmony at any cost? Is this what it means to love and honor your father and mother?"

The answers were similar in many ways.

Compartmentalize

Chuck Griffin responded by saying, "You have to compartmentalize the unconditional love you need to express as you honor them, and separate it from the need to not be victimized by their choices, which may be harmful. Loving does not require accepting."

In his monthly column in *O: The Oprah Magazine*, Dr. Phil McGraw responded to a letter from a woman who was divorced and trying to be a good role model for her children while she navigated a challenging relationship with her ex-husband. Once again, the advice to compartmentalize came up.

> You have to negotiate a new relationship with your ex. You actually have two relationships with him—[yours as the ex-wife and] one in which he is the father of your children. The first one involves a painful history of betrayal, and you need to build a fence around that pain and work on it separately until the hurt is healed. As for the second relationship, you may not like or trust your ex, but he is the only father your children will ever have. If you love your kids, and I know you do, then make it your goal to create a peaceful relationship with their father. Tell yourself, *Only by compartmentalizing my feelings can I reach a resolution about this chapter of my life while protecting my kids.*[2]

I have a friend whose father was a raging alcoholic as she grew up. He's been sober for two decades, but she sometimes has a hard time compartmentalizing the different relationships.

Her early relationship was with the father who drank, and now she has a relationship with the father who is sober. She also has a third relationship with her father as the grandfather of her three children. She's working on building the relationship by compartmentalizing the painful feelings and memories, and defining boundaries has been an important step in her healing. Max Lucado's summation:

> It's dangerous to sum up grand truths in one statement but I'm going to try. If a sentence or two could capture God's desire for each of us it might read like this: God loves you just the way you are, but he refuses to leave you that way. He wants you to be just like Jesus.
>
> God loves you just the way you are. If you think his love for you would be stronger if your faith were, you are wrong. If you think his love would be deeper if your thoughts were, wrong again. Don't confuse God's love with the love of people. The love of people often increases with performance and

decreases with mistakes. Not so with God's love. He loves you right where you are.[3]

When we are in the midst of the stress, burnout, and chaos of trying to do the right thing concerning our aging parents, God loves us, right where we are. Yet He also desires for us to grow. This spiritual growth is critical, so we need to consistently take time to nurture our relationship with Jesus—to maintain our priorities and set spiritual boundaries. Writer and mentor Karen O'Connor knows firsthand about striving to be spiritually and emotionally healthy, as she shows in her response to my survey:

> Even though it's easy to blame the parents for poor choices and bad behavior, my experience with healing my relationship with my parents before they died, and the support I've sought through the anonymous programs, has shown me that I am responsible for myself. No one—not even a parent—can do it to me. If I know who I am in Christ, and carry out my life with self-respect and integrity, then good things will come to me, including healthy relationships. That has been and is currently true for me—but it took me many years to reach this level of health.

An expert in writing humor for seniors, including the bestsellers *Help, Lord! I'm Having a Senior Moment* and *Gettin' Old Ain't for Wimps*, Karen O'Connor has contributed valuable insight as a questionnaire respondent for both *Setting Boundaries* books. She acquired her wisdom through the fires of testing. Like Karen, we may take years to fully experience the power of love and forgiveness.

We need God's help if we are going to learn to love our aging parents even when they are behaving poorly, when they seem utterly unlovable. In Virelle Kidder's response to my survey, she referred to the power of God's love:

> God's love isn't contingent on our capacity to love him back. Once turned lose, it is the only power on earth capable of

changing another human life from the inside out. God calls it grace, totally unmerited love. Receiving grace can be revolutionary. Giving it is God-like.

Your aging parents may not share your walk of faith. This can make things challenging, but God is certainly powerful enough to perform miracles in their lives. Karen O'Connor experienced this firsthand.

> My father stopped speaking to me when I gave my life to Christ and then followed a different religious path than the one he set me on as a child. But by the time my father was in his final stages of illness and near death, he allowed me to pray with him to receive Christ. We healed our relationship and became closer than we had ever been.

> Love is patient, love is kind. It does not envy, it does not boast, it is not proud. It is not rude, it is not self-seeking, it is not easily angered, it keeps no record of wrongs. Love does not delight in evil but rejoices with the truth. It always protects, always trusts, always hopes, always perseveres…And now these three remain: faith, hope and love. But the greatest of these is love.
>
> 1 CORINTHIANS 13:4-7

Scripture teaches us what it means to love. As we continue the journey of setting boundaries with our aging parents, remember, "the greatest of these is love." Never underestimate the power of God to change our lives and the lives of those we love.

Balancing Actions

1. Write the following sentence on a piece of paper and tape it to your bathroom mirror: "Today I will verbally say the words 'I love you' to my parents and to the loved ones with whom I share my life and home."

2. Make a list of all the people you love and take the time to say a prayer for each one.

3. Whom do you most need to forgive?

9

Respect

Many of my fellow baby boomers will remember Aretha Franklin's trademark song "Respect." Although we grew up singing and spelling it, I'm not sure we fully comprehended what it meant—only that Aretha was asking for it and we were dancing to it.

When it comes to healthy boundaries, respect and honor have been greatly misconstrued and misunderstood. Just as honor does not mean to accept without question all negative and harmful behavior, respect is not something we automatically give or receive as though it were genetically programmed, like DNA. It doesn't have anything to do with a statement like this: "I'm your parent, and therefore you need to respect whatever I say or do."

Respecting People's Positions

Respecting people is very different from respecting their positions or roles. The difference is more than semantics, and differentiating between the two is not being hypocritical. For example, when someone becomes the president of the United States, his or her position demands respect regardless of how much I might disapprove of or disagree with the person's opinion or politics. Should I be asked what I personally believe, I will respond with honesty, integrity, and conviction, but I will not overtly and intentionally disparage or disrespect the position of the president of the United States. The role, or position, deserves respect.

In the biblical story of David and Saul, David clearly had a lot of issues with Saul. Yet he recognized Saul was the king regardless of what he did or how he did it. Ray Pritchard writes, "It was not an issue of whether or not Saul treated David right; as long as Saul was the king, he deserved respect by virtue of his position. In particular that meant that David was not free to get even or take revenge in any form."[1] That didn't mean David agreed with Saul or that he sacrificed his ethics and integrity.

In the Army you'll hear the saying, "You don't salute the man, you salute the rank." The colonel may be an absolute jerk, but that doesn't matter; you salute him because of his position. That's precisely the principle here. David owed Saul his respect by virtue of Saul's position as king. Likewise, we owe our parents respect because of their position as our parents.

Respecting People's Boundaries

To respect people means to hold them in high regard and esteem, to value them, and to consider them as deserving. In the questionnaire I distributed, I asked, "Can adult children honor and respect their aging parents while disagreeing with their choices and establishing firm boundaries with them? If so, how?"

Virtually every respondent said yes. However, the overriding caveat was that, for the children to set firm boundaries, the aging parents must be able to cognitively understand their choices. If your aging parents are unable to understand right from wrong, the dynamics of setting and maintaining boundaries change. But let's continue to assume our aging parents understand their choices—and those choices have been harmful to us for a long time. When people consistently behave negatively, they foster disrespect. We can respect a role—a position—but feel conflicted about respecting the person.

A time may come when we must disconnect from our parents because of this difference. Should this occur, we must express our feelings in love and honor. In some cases, this will require a Herculean effort—and nothing less than God's amazing grace and mercy.

Rebecca loved her parents, yet the older her mother got, the more cruel and disrespectful she became toward her husband, Rebecca's father.

"Dad would brush her off, seeming to ignore her when she criticized him or dishonored him. Maybe that's what you do after 60 years of marriage, I don't know. But it killed me to sit by and listen to her berate him. For the longest time, I tried to stand up for Dad, but that wasn't my place, and I caused even more problems, so I had to stop that.

"But D-day came when I noticed how disrespectfully our two young daughters were beginning to speak to us—to my husband and me—and I suddenly realized they were learning this from their grandmother. We explained to our girls how God wants us to treat others and that sometimes even grown-ups make mistakes—that we needed to respect and love Grandma, but that we felt she was wrong in yelling at Grandpa.

"Eventually, we had to lay down the law, to set a firm boundary with my mother. We told her that what she did in her own home was her choice, but when she and Dad were in our home and around our children, she could not speak to their grandpa, her husband, in such a disrespectful way. We told her if it happened again we would immediately point it out, hold her accountable, and ask her to leave. Our daughters needed to learn what was right behavior."

Rebecca and her husband discussed the consequences of this action, firm in their resolve not to give in. They prayed their mother would understand eventually and change her behavior, but if she did not, that would be her choice.

"Our job as parents is to protect our children—to teach them. We did what we felt was right, but it wasn't easy."

They knew this might disconnect them from Rebecca's parents for a time, and although they prayed for the best-case scenario, they were prepared for the worst-case scenario.

"Holding her accountable caused some problems at first, but eventually Mom learned that we were serious. She's on her best behavior at our home, and I know my dad is much happier."

⸙

We can love and honor our aging parents, even though we may disagree with them, as Chuck Griffin affirms in his response to my survey:

> Sometimes we have to take control of our lives and firmly and lovingly express to our parents that while they may choose a certain pathway, we cannot follow in it for whatever reason, and then be firm in our resolve. It may be the example they need to turn around. They may never agree with us, yet it is the course we need to follow to remain sane.

It's important to note that asking someone to respect our boundaries is not the same as asking someone to respect us. There is a difference. It's a sad fact of life that there is a chance your parents may never respect the person you are. Your differences could be too vast, the chasm between your lives too wide. This does not mean you don't deserve their respect; it just means that for whatever reason, your aging parents are unable to give it.

Therefore, we cannot demand that someone respect us. We can, however, demand that someone respect the boundaries we set to protect us and those we love. If that were not the case, why bother to set them at all?

Consequences

So we can't require people to respect us, but we can require them to respect our position and our boundaries. But this brings up another question: "How do we follow through?" We can expect and require and demand that people respect our boundaries until we are blue in the face, but the truth is, we can't *make* people comply.

Here's the answer: We can clearly explain what will happen if they don't. We can set the consequences.

When we consistently follow through and enforce boundaries, we must be prepared for others to break the rules. When that happens, we need to be ready to enforce the consequences. It's true, your aging parents may never respect you, but in time they will come to respect the boundary choices you have made if you consistently and lovingly enforce them.

> The LORD himself goes before you and will be with you; he will never leave you nor forsake you. Do not be afraid; do not be discouraged.
>
> DEUTERONOMY 31:8

As we have seen, some parents' thoughts, attitudes, and behaviors may be so toxic that respecting any people, positions, or boundaries is difficult for them. This may be a bitter pill for us to swallow as adult children because we desperately want our parents to love and respect us. When they don't, we can feel crushed. This is when it's vital to remember that our Father God will never harm us—that He alone can bring us the peace and balance we need.

Self-Respect

While it's important for others to respect the boundaries we have established, it's equally important to have self-respect. Having self-respect is not the same as being selfish.

When we peel back the layers of everything that has occurred to bring us to this point, including all of the dynamics that make us who we are, there is a basic truth at the core of every child of God, a synergistic component that binds us all together: We are all made in the image of God. As children of the King, we have great worth, inestimable value.

The Old Testament teaches us that we were created in the image of God. And the New Testament reveals that our hearts and minds are being reshaped to reflect God's own image.

Every human being is worthy of respect because we are all made in the image of God. Our parents are also worthy of that same level of respect because they too are made in God's image.

⁓

Ethel was 92 years old when I met her. Sharp as a tack and a joy to be around, I looked forward to seeing her when I visited my mom. A God-fearing woman, the wisdom she possessed was more valuable than rare gemstones.

Ethel knew I was a writer (my mom told anyone who would listen), and she always spoke to me as though I had a column in the *New York Times* read by millions. Mutual respect abounded.

She was sad the last time I saw her. The light in her eyes had disappeared, and my heart ached for her. "My body gave out years ago, but that doesn't mean I'm an imbecile. Write that down, honey. I'm not an imbecile." (Almost everyone on my mother's floor who was cognitive called me honey).

Mom told me why Ethel was so sad.

"Her son and his newest wife were here a few days ago," Mom said, shaking her head and frowning, "They want to build a new house."

> Do not lie to each other, since you have taken off your old self with its practices and have put on the new self, which is being renewed in knowledge in the image of its Creator. Here there is no Greek or Jew, circumcised or uncircumcised, barbarian, Scythian, slave or free, but Christ is all, and is in all.
>
> COLOSSIANS 3:9-11

Mom rarely judged people out loud, but you knew her opinion if you were in the same room with her. She wasn't one to clearly articulate her feelings or to disparage someone with hearsay or gossip, but her body language and subtle innuendos spoke volumes. She clearly did not approve of Ethel's son and daughter-in-law.

I recalled that Ethel's son had recently refurbished the family home.

It was an estate, actually. The home had been in Ethel's family for generations, a massive Tudor on the Lake Erie Gold Coast. Ethel lived there with her son and his family until she got sick and came to the nursing home. She hoped to return one day and often talked about dying in the same place that she'd been born.

"Okay, so they want to build a house. What's wrong with that?" I asked.

"He wants to sell Ethel's home to get the money to do it."

Apparently the son had said something like this: "You're probably never going to leave this place and go back there to live, and I know you left me the house in your will, so I'd like to sell it now and use the money to build something newer on a couple of acres that we're looking at in the country." He even had a buyer for Ethel's home already lined up. Ethel simply needed to sign it over to him, and he'd take care of the rest. But she was crushed that he would ask such a thing.

This son knew his mother longed to return to the home of her youth. Even if he suspected this might never happen, it wasn't his place to accelerate the timeline. This is a clear example of blatant disrespect.

> If one doesn't respect oneself, one can have neither love nor respect for others.
>
> AYN RAND

Not surprisingly, Ethel wouldn't agree to the request. An argument ensued, and her son and his wife had apparently left in a huff with talk about seeing a lawyer to have Ethel declared incompetent to handle her affairs. But Ethel was as competent as anyone I know. Clearly this son and his wife had their own agenda, and the way they had handled the situation was obviously disrespectful.

Do you remember Cloud and Townsend's laws of boundaries we mentioned earlier?

The Ten Laws of Boundaries

the law of sowing and reaping

the law of responsibility

the law of power

the law of respect

the law of motivation

the law of evaluation

the law of proactivity

the law of envy

the law of activity

the law of exposure[2]

The law of respect is based primarily on Jesus' teaching in Matthew 7:12: "So in everything, do to others what you would have them do to you."

Balancing Actions

1. Write in your journal what respect means to you.

2. Identify ways you can help your aging parents feel respected.

3. Do you respect yourself? If so, how do you demonstrate self-respect? If not, how can you build self-respect?

4. Are you a mom or a dad yourself? Respect the positions everyone holds in your family and honor your family today by spending time together.

10

When Your Parents Become Dependent

People live longer than they used to. Your parents may be in better shape than you! As we discussed earlier, some aging parents are active, vital, and able to function independently well into their nineties and beyond. Some even outlive their own children.

On the other hand, you may have been seeing your aging parents' health decline for some time. Clearly defined boundaries are even more critical when your parents become dependent, even if the process is just beginning. This is a season of serious choices as Smick in *Eldercare for the Christian Family* says:

> There is no one formula for choosing appropriate caregiving roles. There are reasonable and circumstantial factors such as geographical proximity, giftedness, emotional strength, age, task orientation, and the aged parent's choice or preference. There are also unhealthy reasons that can enter into the selection process as well, resulting in damaging consequences.
>
> Some aged parents place unreasonable demands on their caregivers. Sometimes these caregivers, because of their own complex feelings towards their parents, place unreasonable demands on themselves. In their zeal, they insist on handling the entire responsibility singlehandedly and discourage anyone else from sharing in it in any way. Eventually, those who

freely offer to help, feel shut out after repeated rejections. It is at this point the caregiver/martyr begins to complain bitterly to anyone who will listen about the heavy burdens and the selfishness of her family. Truly the aging parent can become a pawn in family power struggles.[1]

If we have established a pattern of open communication with our parents and our siblings, this new season can bring sweet expressions of love and respect. If, however, communication is strained or virtually non-existent, it can bring seemingly unmanageable stress and burnout.

It's important to remember that we must respect our parents' ability to make their own decisions for as long as they possibly can. We should not impose our own agendas on them. If they gradually become less competent, this might be a bit challenging, especially if they are toxic or stubborn to a fault. Eventually, they may be unable to see the big picture and make decisions in their best interest, or they may turn the dependency corner and no longer be cognitively aware of what's best for them. Wherever your parents are in their decline toward dependence, use all the love and grace you can muster as you help them through this role reversal. Whenever possible, approach it with prayer and rational thinking, not with purely emotional reactions.

Knowing in your spirit the right thing to do is good. Embracing wholeheartedly God's standards, which He established for your well-being, is also good. Feeling obligated, feeling as if you have no choice, and doing something that will damage and perhaps even destroy your heart or the heart of someone over whom you have stewardship...these are not good.

You do have choices when your parents become increasingly dependent, and God will surely honor the choices you make after a great deal of thought, prayer, reflection, and wise counsel. Smick continues:

> When an older person begins to lose the ability to manage independently, concerned relatives too often think of only two options: 1) assuming the responsibility of total care themselves, or 2) placing the older person in a nursing home.

In practical terms, the option of assuming the responsibility of total care in your home is not realistic for many families today. Today's housing is built for the nuclear family, not the extended family. With 54 percent of women entering today's work force, the majority of households no longer have a full-time primary caretaker who can provide all the services an elderly parent in failing health might need. In addition, the habits of independent living, formed over so many years, might be very difficult for both the aging parents and their children to break. Although some adult children feel a responsibility to take their aging parents into their own homes, many simply cannot. And many older people would prefer not to be dependent on their children in any case.[2]

Since *Eldercare for the Christian Family* was written in 1990, that figure of 54 percent has raised to 59.5 percent—approximately 72 million women are part of the workforce in America. Women are the primary caregivers in most homes where aging parents reside, so giving the parents the level of care they may need can be difficult. As Smick indicates, life today is different than it was for earlier generations.

If your parent becomes increasingly dependent, you have several options. Begin discussing these with your parents as soon as possible. Here is Smick's idea:

It takes courage to wade into the potentially turbulent waters of a discussion with your parent about his or her health, housing, financial, or legal matters. There is no guarantee that your overtures will be well received—but it is possible that you'll discover your loved one also wanted to talk about these concerns. He or she just didn't know how to start the conversation. While it is seldom easy and sometimes painful, important information and feelings can be shared in these discussions. If they are properly handled, misunderstandings and uncertainties are less likely to get in the way of the good of everyone in the family. How we communicate with our parents will also have an impact on how we feel about ourselves for having made the effort to care in a Christ-honoring way.[3]

There are plenty of things to talk about when our aging parents become dependent. As I mentioned earlier, countless resources are available to assist you in this journey regarding your parents' health, medical conditions, legal issues, nursing-home options, home health care, and the like.

It is impossible to address all the concerns you may have as a full- or part-time caregiver, whether living locally or far away. But I can address your need to keep your sanity, to remember your priorities and motivation, and to clearly establish your boundaries in love, honor, and respect.

What We Can Control

As much as possible, be prepared and do not make rash decisions based on emotional responses. Look closely at your situation to determine what you can and cannot control as well as what you should and should not control. Diane Viere commented on this in response to my survey:

> Having a clear understanding of what we can and cannot control is essential. Additionally, it is important for the adult children as caregivers to remember that they cannot make everything perfect. The transition from independence to dependence challenges deeply held beliefs and expectations for the parent as well as the adult children. For me, a particularly difficult challenge was my expectation that I could control my parent's outcome if I just worked hard enough, researched and networked long enough, and applied the same principles that had worked all of my adult life. Oh, I could make a difference while advocating for my parent, but I could not make her independent again. Once I accepted that I needed to change my goal, that frustration eased and I began to accept what I did not think I could accept.
>
> Instead of micromanaging my parent's medical needs, emotional changes, and physical limitations—all with the expectation that she would return to independence—I began to look at her transition realistically. My goal then changed,

and I could more effectively care for her needs with a reason-able expectation of comfort, dignity, and love. This discovery unleashed a world of freedom for me.

Chuck Griffin offered this response:

At some point the aging parent may regress to a place where they start becoming childlike in their ability to make deci-sions and in their understanding of situations. I think at that moment we need to gently make the transition from adult child to caregiver and guardian, watching out for their safety and well-being. It will be tough because they may come and go in and out of recognition and ability to make certain deci-sions, and we need to allow them the freedom to make the decisions they are capable of making that are not harmful. An example would be the day we need to take their driving privileges away. It may be the day we can't allow them to climb the basement stairs. It may be the day we can't trust them to use the stove and we order Meals on Wheels so they get good nutrition.

The bottom line is affirming them in all their current abilities while expressing your love for them and relaying concerns for their safety. I think it's all about dialogue and choosing our words carefully so they get the impression they are in control and are making the decisions. So instead of taking away their keys, we talk about the feelings they would have if they were in an accident and hurt someone.

As I said earlier in the chapter, it's a season of serious choices. Smick concurs:

In most cases, a child's need for assistance in the activities of daily living is only temporary and moves rapidly towards the child's delighted self-discovery of independence. The elderly, however, are moving in the opposite direction on the independence scale and have increasing needs for assistance every day.

The child knows no world outside the one parents provide; aging parents, on the other hand, often bring into our homes a perspective on the world that differs greatly from our own, sometimes accompanied by a disapproval of the lifestyle we have chosen.

Although caregivers suffer much self-inflicted guilt, parents themselves can be outstanding inducers of guilt. Gerontologists know that certain personality traits, even the unfavorable ones, can become more pronounced as a senior gets older.[4]

Whether your aging parent is a lion or a lamb, the journey to dependency is one that you can travel lovingly and efficiently if you plan in advance and have a roadmap. Making sudden, emotional responses when things get difficult is a lot like being lost on a road trip. You can find yourself making wrong turns and desperately going in circles without making any discernable headway toward your destination.

Why do we get caught up in the insanity? We can't pretend that we don't know our parents are getting older. Talk with your parents soon so the trip can be as enjoyable as possible and focused on what really matters—authentic love, honor, and respect. Your parents deserve this, as do you.

Balancing Actions

1. Have your parents shown signs of increasing dependency on you or others?

2. What issues, if any, do you foresee as potentially problematic as your parents age?

3. How can you create a roadmap to help you better address those issues?

11

Financial Fallout

Years before I gave my heart to the Lord, Pink Floyd's album *Dark Side of the Moon* was on the top of the rock charts. It was a favorite of mine, and I listened to it all the time. One track on the album was titled "Money," and it began with the sound of a cash register and clanking coins, accompanied by a hard-pounding beat and a rather foreboding laugh. Unbeknownst to me, this particular song brought abject terror into the heart of my son, who was a very young boy at the time. "I used to hide under the covers when I heard it, I was so scared of that laugh—that song," he told me years later. I had no idea.

The same can be said about many of us dealing with money and finances today. We're scared to death and want nothing more than to hide under the covers.

Money is a significant part of the enabling dynamic affecting our adult children today. I often tell parents that love is not spelled m-o-n-e-y. We've confused the two.

⁓

"What do you mean you're overdrawn $2500 in your checking account?" Gloria was stunned at her mother's announcement.

"I don't know, I guess I forgot to enter the withdrawals when I used that infernal debit card thingy! I told you I didn't want that card, but you made me..."

"Hold on, Mom," Gloria's husband interrupted. "Don't blame Gloria for this. Using a debit card was easier for you than writing checks, remember? We talked about this."

"I don't care, it's no good. I can't remember to write down where I use it."

"You can't remember where you spent $2500?" Gloria shouted.

Gloria's mother had recently discovered two new things: the local casino and the easily accessible ATMs positioned strategically near the slot machines. This became a serious problem—even more so when Gloria and her husband refused to cover the overdrafts and fees.

⌇

The lack of financial boundaries has wreaked havoc on families today. Financial stress is the number one cause of divorce in our country and plays a significant role in depression, alcoholism, and even suicide. No wonder Scripture tells it like it is about money matters: "The love of money is a root of all kinds of evil. Some people, eager for money, have wandered from the faith and pierced themselves with many griefs" (1 Timothy 6:10). Note that money isn't evil; rather, our *love* of money causes the problems.

> Where your treasure is, there your heart will be also.
>
> MATTHEW 6:21

Remember that personal property lines define who we are and influence all areas of our lives. Let's review the primary types of boundaries again:

physical

mental

emotional

financial

spiritual

Finance is one of the topics we seem to consistently shuffle to the bottom of the stack, always waiting for a better time to discuss it. But of course, that time never seems to arrive. That is, until we have no other choice.

"Parents of the baby boomer generation, as a whole, keep things very, very close to the vest," says Kenneth Kamen, president of Mercadien Asset Management. "This is a patriarchal generation. The guys who came back from (World War II) didn't want to talk to anyone about anything. It's amazing how little the baby boomers know about the financial situation of their parents."

Discussing these matters with family members *before* a crisis forces your hand is always the best way. If you're married, talk with your spouse about how much you can afford to help. Make this important decision together.

Earlier I said that loaning your parents money isn't always wrong. The problem comes when they never repay the loan or when the help you offer your parents starts to become a serious hardship for you, threatening your ability to care for your own immediate family.

The first step in sanity is to stop our negative behavior. A second "stop step" follows close on its heals: Stop the flow of money. Remember how many of the earlier examples concerned money? Virtually all of them: the young man who bought a car for his father, the couple who paid their mother's rent, the man who helped his parents budget and supplemented their income, and Gloria's mother's gambling problem.

Buying Love

It's not always about adult children coming to their parents' rescue with money. Some aging parents have a great deal of money, and they use it to powerfully control their children. Such was the case in Betty's family. The argument reached critical mass when Betty's mother shouted over the phone:

"That boy is ungrateful, and he's selfish. I only asked him to drive me to the nursery so I could get some plant food, but you'd have thought I was asking for blood! Who pays for his guitar lessons? Who just bought new speakers for your TV room? It's the least he could do."

Her mother called virtually every day to ask Betty or one of her teenagers to do something for her, and they often dropped everything to accommodate her requests, but it was getting out of control. Every gift she gave came with strings attached, and those strings were beginning to strangle everyone in Betty's family.

Money can also cause some adult children to be greedy and disrespectful. (Remember Ethel's son and daughter-in-law, who wanted to declare her incompetent so they could sell her family home?) Dependence on parents' money can also foster a host of other dysfunctions in a family. Things can get out of balance when we give and or receive money for the wrong reasons. Cloud and Townsend share a perfect example:

> Terry and Sherri were an attractive couple. They owned a big house and went on lavish vacations; their children took piano lessons and ballet, and they had their own skis, rollerblades, ice skates, and windsurfers. Terry and Sherri had all the trappings of success. But there was one problem. This lifestyle was not supported by Terry's paycheck. Terry and Sherri received much financial help from his family.

> Terry's family had always wanted the best for him, and they had always helped him get it. They had contributed to the house, the vacations, and the children's hobbies. While this allowed Terry and Sherri to have things they could not otherwise have, it cost them dearly as well.

> The periodic bailouts from his parents cut into Terry's self-respect. And Sherri felt as if she couldn't spend any money without consulting her in-laws, since they contributed the funds.

> Terry illustrates a common boundary problem for young adults today, both married and single: He was not yet an adult financially. He could not set boundaries on his parents' desire for him and Sherri to "have everything we have." He

also found that he had so fused with their ideas of success that he had trouble saying no to these wishes in himself. He wasn't sure he wanted to forsake the gifts and handouts for a greater sense of independence.

Terry's story is the "up" side of the financial boundary problem. There is also the "I'm in trouble" side. Many adult children perpetually get into financial messes because of irresponsibility, drug or alcohol use, out-of-control spending, or the modern "I haven't found my niche" syndrome. Their parents continue to finance this road of failure and irresponsibility, thinking that "this time they'll do better." In reality, they are crippling their children for life, preventing them from achieving independence.

An adult who does not stand on his own financially is still a child. To be an adult, you must live within your means and pay for your own failures.[1]

In her book *The Overwhelmed Woman's Guide to Caring for Aging Parents*, Julie-Allyson Ieron tells the story of a group of siblings who worked together to successfully address a host of issues surrounding the care of their widowed mother and even develop a written contract that identified all aspects of the arrangement. This document ensured that all siblings were on the same page, leaving no room for personal interpretation of verbal agreements, which can sometimes be misconstrued or misunderstood. Financial responsibilities factored significantly in this document.

This family was able to come together with one common goal— to love and honor not only their parents but also one another. They appointed one sibling to take notes and type up the agreement, and they hashed out every detail imaginable. The family is six years into the arrangement, and all parties are content with its fairness.

Adult children are juggling so many tasks, it's almost impossible to remember everything without keeping some kind of written record. From grocery lists to detailed Day-Timers, we have grown accustomed to recording important aspects of daily life. Consider including this habit when you develop plans for your aging parents, and particularly when finances are involved.

When complex emotions and decisions are added to the mix, and especially when siblings are involved, putting things in writing is even more important. Nothing about this is insensitive or cruel. Quite the opposite, in fact; a document gives everyone who is involved a clear picture of what is happening, and it greatly diminishes the likelihood of anyone having false assumptions. We'll talk more about what to write in a later chapter.

Money can cause a great deal of stress when our parents become increasingly dependent and we need to begin potentially uncomfortable discussions with them and our siblings about their future. If we don't address this issue, the stress can escalate catastrophically.

Financial boundaries can be the most difficult to set. Don't hesitate to seek counsel from a trusted advisor, and be certain to put your plan in writing.

Balancing Actions

1. What is your earliest memory of money?

2. What financial boundary could you implement immediately that would help alleviate some stress?

3. Do you have an advance directive and a will? Have you decided how your funeral arrangements should be handled, put your wishes in writing, and shared them with your family? If not, develop these vital documents soon.

Part Two

The Six Steps to SANITY

In *Setting Boundaries with Your Adult Children,* I offered the Six Steps to SANITY as a prescription to a host of illnesses. This analogy also holds true in dealing with aging parents. The Six Steps to SANITY outlined in the following chapters will help us cure our illness of poor boundary setting, deal with the symptoms of burnout, and reveal why we need to guard our hearts.

> Above all else, guard your heart, for it is the wellspring of life.
>
> PROVERBS 4:23

One dose of this medicine won't do it; we'll need to stay on this prescription for quite some time until we return to full health. By then, the Six Steps to SANITY will have become second nature. In fact, you'll be surprised by the way they apply to virtually every decision you make.

In addition to our six-step prescription, we must take daily doses of prayer to maintain our resolve to make changes. We don't want to lose the momentum we have gained by making positive changes. Therefore, we must continue on this prescription for the duration of the treatment—regardless of how difficult it may be.

I must caution you, however, that this treatment may bring long-term side effects: You will likely begin to regain your sanity, build self-respect, and develop your relationship with the Lord.

So what exactly is sanity?

Sanity is what we gain when we shift our priorities, when we stop focusing on other people's problems, stop fixating on the situations and circumstances of life, and begin to concentrate on changing our own attitudes and behaviors.

Setting Boundaries

+ The Six Steps to SANITY

+ Praying
_____

= Balance and Self-respect

This bears repeating: This shift in our priorities is not a generic excuse to jettison our aging parents into a black hole, where they must fend for themselves regardless of what happens. (Of course, some toxic parents may benefit from fending for themselves for a while.) This shift in priorities is not intended to promote selfishness.

The Six Steps to SANITY empower us to guard our hearts, get right with God, and gain wisdom to make rational choices in all areas of our lives—to set healthy boundaries so we can truly help ourselves, our families, and our parents in authentic and loving ways.

Remember, we don't want to implement boundaries that will cause us regrets after our parents have left this earth. Death may eventually end a life, but it does not end a relationship. We want the memories from this season of life to be as loving and authentic as possible under whatever circumstances. We want to honestly say we did our best. However, your best is different from mine. Don't judge yourself by comparing your abilities or achievements with someone else's.

The Six Steps to SANITY will help us in any situation. We can implement them when our aging parents...

live independently	live in a nursing home
live with us	are in prison or jail
live with another relative	are believers (or not)
live in assisted living	are toxic

In short, the Six Steps to SANITY work in any scenario because they don't focus on the situations or circumstances in life. They show us how to respond to them.

I trust by now you've begun to realize the part you have played in contributing to your state of burnout as well as the enemy's tactics in using these negative feelings against you. I also pray you have realized the futility of harboring the negative feelings of guilt, frustration, anger, fear, and inadequacy—and that you are ready to develop new strengths to begin living a life of freedom. It's time for healing—emotionally, spiritually, financially, physically, and psychologically. It's time to find sanity!

SIX STEPS TO SANITY

S = Stop your own negative behaviors (and especially stop the flow of money!).

A = Assemble a support group.

N = Nip excuses in the bud.

I = Implement rules and boundaries.

T = Trust your instincts.

Y = Yield everything to God (let go and let God).

12

S—*Stop* Your Own Negative Behavior

Most of us adult children have the best intentions when we try to help our parents. But as difficult as it may be to hear, in our desire to help, we may have been doing things for them that they can and should be doing for themselves—things that can keep them engaged in life. We have sometimes inadvertently robbed them of their dignity and self-respect. We have violated our aging parents' boundaries.

Many of us adult children take on too much responsibility. This is one of the boundary violations that contribute to our stress and burnout. On the other hand, many of our aging parents have violated our boundaries, and this also adds stress. Life presents plenty of difficult circumstances or situations, and our parents' personalities, behaviors, attitudes, and choices don't make things any easier. As we've discussed, some aging parents are indeed toxic, wreaking havoc wherever they go. Their actions and our own feelings of powerlessness and inability to set limits have conspired to rob us of our own dignity and self-respect.

We have overstepped some of their boundaries, and they have overstepped some of ours. Sometimes, the two happen at the same time. Whatever the case may be, if your life has become less peaceful and more painful, it's time to say, "Enough is enough." It's time to stop.

Based on my experience and from feedback I have received from psychologists and counselors, you must take four critical "stop steps" in order to forever end the insanity that causes stress and leads to burnout—steps that will help you turn your life around:

1. Stop repeating your own negative behavior.
2. Stop ignoring your own personal issues.
3. Stop being alone in your pain.
4. Stop the flow of money.

1. Stop Repeating Your Own Negative Behavior

Talk is cheap.

It's one thing to say we'll stop enabling our parents, stop allowing toxic parents to infect our lives, stop being rude and disrespectful to our parents, or stop ignoring our own needs as if they didn't matter. It's another thing entirely to commit to change and to do the necessary work to embark on a journey of self-discovery and self-respect.

To implement the Six Steps to SANITY, we must make a decision with a great deal of prayer and discussion with our spouse and support group accountability partner. But first, we must be fully convinced that we need to stop repeating our own enabling behaviors. We must be ready, willing, and able to commit wholeheartedly to the process of change. We must be prepared for the inevitable storms to come. We'll stand strong in our commitment to stop only if we think through it carefully and commit to it fully.

In her book *The Emotionally Destructive Relationship*, Leslie Vernick addressed the truth about change and the way change begins when our negative behaviors stop.

> I hope you see by now how lying to yourself is so detrimental to your well-being. When we habitually deceive ourselves, we cannot grow or mature in a godly way. As painful as truth can be, we must face it if we want to become healthy, no matter how much we don't like what it tells us.
>
> Recently a woman e-mailed me about her experience:
>
> > I believe that getting out of a destructive situation has

nothing to do with recognizing that the other person is abusive or that we are not safe, or in getting the other person to change. I believe that I began to change when I realized that my life was spiraling downward and I felt hopeless. I realized that the choices I'd made over and over again were not getting me closer to joy but were taking me further and further down a destructive road. Recovery came for me when *I decided that I needed to change,* and that I was the only person I could affect or change, and that I couldn't do this alone. I needed God…

The most painful step in any healing process is often the first one. You must face the ugly truth that you're in a destructive relationship and that you are the one who has allowed it to continue. Just like a person wouldn't begin chemo-therapy unless she first accepted that she has cancer, you will not take the steps necessary to grow, heal, or change if you are still in denial. As long as you minimize the truth about your problem, you cannot become strong enough to challenge or change anything…

> Every prudent man acts out of knowledge, but a fool exposes his folly.
>
> **PROVERBS 13:16**

Wherever you are, it is important you realize that stopping the destructive dance starts with you.[1]

The change starts with us. This is critical: we must stop repeating our own negative behavior. To expect change without this step would be foolish.

2. Stop Ignoring Your Personal Issues

When I checked myself into a one-month treatment program years ago to sort out the mess I had made of my own life, I finally began to see my destructive behaviors (especially the way I enabled others) for what they were.

There are so many extenuating circumstances as to why we do the things we do, and so many intricate components to how we've arrived at this place in life. However, in my experience there appears to be a common theme in the overall pathology of enabling…and that theme is the general neglect of our own hearts. Whether it's a relatively minor issue that needs to be addressed or a major malady, the fact tends to be global that in focusing so much time and energy on the problems of [others], we have neglected the issues that have made us who we are today. We must be willing to look inwardly at ourselves to identify our reasons for allowing things to get so out of hand. We cannot begin to implement the changes that need to occur if we aren't willing to recognize the part we play in the drama.[2]

> Blessed is the man who trusts in the LORD, whose confidence is in him.
>
> JEREMIAH 17:7

In part 1, we discussed many personal issues that can lead to burnout, including these:

We don't understand our place within the family of God.

We have not made our spiritual health a key priority.

We've lost sight of our priorities in general.

We've neglected to define our personal boundaries.

We think we don't have a choice.

Our own destructive patterns get in the way.

Our motivations have been wrong.

We do too much for others.

We don't focus on our own health and well-being.

We may also be headed for burnout because we have not yet learned to trust in God for the outcome. At some point, every Christian adult will have to release his or her parents to God and learn to trust Him for whatever happens.

Perhaps you need to acknowledge other personal issues. Think about it. Pray about it. What must you deal with in your own life at this time? Whatever the trial, rest assured that God will not give you more than you can handle. This is not merely a Christian platitude—it is God's truth. We must stop ignoring our own personal issues.

3. Stop Being Alone in Your Pain

The international SANITY Support Group Network grew from a seed God planted in my heart as I wrote *Setting Boundaries with Your Adult Children*. During my season as a new believer, I didn't tell others about my situation with my son. I believed (wrongly) that good Christian parents didn't have children who were involved in drugs, crime, and a host of other behaviors that made my life chaotic, crazy, and insane. In time, I realized I was wrong.

> Blessed is the man who perseveres under trial, because when he has stood the test, he will receive the crown of life that God has promised to those who love him.
>
> JAMES 1:12

> For too long we've felt like outcasts in a world of perfect parents and perfect kids, when in reality there are families just like ours all around us. Parents in pain exist in our church home, in our workplace, and in our neighborhood—often suffering in silence. Support groups such as Al-Anon, Co-Dependents Anonymous and Six-Steps to SANITY support groups meet in locations around the country. Joining, or in some cases starting, a support group is vital.
>
> Professional therapy might be the best way to go when we need to make significant changes in our life. Having the benefit of an objective opinion and the therapeutic advice of a professional is invaluable. In addition to professional counseling on an hourly or sliding-scale pay basis, there are many resources available to us at little or no cost. We may have to conduct a bit of research to find them—but it will be worth it. For many of us, it's much too difficult to heal without objective, qualified, and nonjudgmental help.[3]

It's important not to isolate yourself during this time of change. With more than 37.3 million seniors in our country, you can rest assured you aren't alone in your struggle to balance your relationship with your aging parents with the other areas of concern in your life. We were created to be in relationship—with God the Father and with other brothers and sisters in Christ. We must stop being alone in our pain.

4. Stop the Flow of Money

When we have poor boundaries, we almost always pour out our money for those we love. Whether it's $20 or $20,000, we must stop coming to our parents' rescue or buying their love with our checkbooks. Our money is often a life preserver that buoys up our dysfunctional relationships and keeps them afloat through yet another storm. This too must stop.

I'm blessed to call Thelma Wells a dear friend—a true sister in Christ. A gifted author, speaker, professor, and Bible teacher, she is the president of Women of God Ministries. You may know Thelma (aka Mama T) from her years with the Women of Faith organization, where she spoke to arenas of 50,000 women or more.

But you may not know that God has led Thelma to say goodbye to Women of Faith and to embark on a new journey. The Ready to Win tour kicked off in 2009 at the Garland, Texas, convention center, and I was blessed to be one of Thelma's keynote speakers. We have had several Ready to Win events since, and I am amazed at the way God moves each time I share the Six Steps to SANITY.

> I tell you that if two of you on earth agree about anything you ask for, it will be done for you by my Father in heaven. For where two or three come together in my name, there am I with them.
>
> MATTHEW 18:19-20

For example, at the end of the Garland conference, a tearful yet exuberant mother grabbed my hands as she came up to me on the concourse.

"God bless you!" she cried. "I wasn't going to come today because I had another fight with my adult son this morning. I've had it with his lifestyle, and I've had it being used. He wanted to borrow $40, and I told him no. I'm struggling to make ends meet, and I'm sick of supporting his cigarette habit, his partying, and his lazy lifestyle."

I nodded, fully understanding her turmoil, but also intrigued at why she was bubbling over. I sensed her "Holy Spirit hallelujah halo"—an aura of joy that could not be contained.

"When you said we need to stop the flow of money, God spoke to me! He told me to give the $40 I didn't give to my son to Thelma and her ministry—to sow a seed where it will really help. I just came from her booth. I gave her the $40. I know it's not a lot, but it is for me. I haven't tithed in so long, I forgot how it feels to give from a place of love. Thank you, Allison, thank you."

⁂

We are stewards of our lives and everything we have, including our money. God orchestrated a powerful lesson for this sister in Christ, a lesson that set her free from bondage.

Thelma is no stranger to watching God set people free. She commented on my experience in her response to my survey:

> This precious lady at the Ready to Win Conference heard the words that set her free from enabling her son. She was drawn to the conference because this was the way God had planned to give her sweet relief and free her from keeping her head in the sand of denial and guilt. She was free to stop enabling her adult child, and she was free to think of something larger than her personal issues with her son. I understand her dilemma because whether the child is wayward or for other reasons, *rescue* is our middle name. Or at least it was

my middle name. Now I thank God for Allison's boldness in standing up and telling the truth about our unspoken addictions—and our need for sanity. The lady at the conference really got it. She is a winner because of her brave and prudent decision to stop her own negative behavior and to stop the flow of money. She was definitely Ready to Win!

Our self-respect takes a hit when we give or receive money for the wrong reasons. But our heart reaps great reward when we sow from a place of love. Therefore, as you start changing by stopping, consider where you need to stop the flow of money.

> Remember this: Whoever sows sparingly will also reap sparingly, and whoever sows generously will also reap generously. Each man should give what he has decided in his heart to give, not reluctantly or under compulsion, for God loves a cheerful giver. And God is able to make all grace abound to you, so that in all things at all times, having all that you need, you will abound in every good work.
>
> 2 CORINTHIANS 9:6-8

Change Starts When We Stop

This first of the Six Steps to SANITY will be one of the most difficult, but these four "stop steps" are critical to healing. The first step in any journey of growth is difficult, but without this crucial first step, we'll never arrive at our destination.

Remember again the oft-quoted definition of insanity: repeating the same behavior and expecting different results. Now is the time to stop repeating the behavior that has not produced the desired results. It's time to stop destructive habits and patterns, and start charting a firm and focused course that will help you avoid burnout and build mutual respect.

Once we finally own up to our negative behavior for what it is and recognize the damage it's caused, we won't be able to just pick up where we left off. God willing, we will feel a deep conviction in our soul to make changes, to stop our negative behavior. Yet regardless of how angry we may be, no matter how broken our hearts, we must act in love. Sometimes we need other supportive people around to help us do that—people who understand what we are going through and can lead us to the second step to sanity.

Balancing Actions

1. List the ineffective behaviors you need to stop.
2. Prayerfully prioritize this list.

As a reminder to stop your own negative behavior, photocopy the list on page 144 and put it in a place where you'll see it often, such as your refrigerator door, bulletin board, or bedroom mirror.

THE FIRST STEP TO SANITY:
I WILL *STOP* MY OWN NEGATIVE BEHAVIOR

1. Stop repeating the same responses and expecting different results.

2. Stop ignoring my own personal issues.

3. Stop being alone in my pain.

4. Stop the flow of money—now.

5. Stop pretending things are going to be fine if I continue doing what I have been.

6. Stop putting off the changes I must make.

7. Stop my own destructive patterns and behaviors.

8. Stop feeling guilty.

9. Stop demanding that my aging parents change.

10. Stop making excuses for other people's negative behavior and choices.

11. Stop engaging in arguments, debates, or negotiations (no verbal volleyball).

12. Stop being a martyr.

13

A—*Assemble* a Support Group

Anytime we're embarking on a journey of significant personal change and growth, we need support, understanding, encouragement, and accountability from others who have traveled a similar journey and come out on the other side—or those who are currently walking the journey with us. We may also need a willing individual to stand with us and intercede on our behalf during times of crisis.

When we think of support groups, we usually think of such well-known 12-step groups as Alcoholics Anonymous, Al-Anon, and Celebrate Recovery, which deal primarily with substance abuse. But today, support groups come in all sizes and varieties and deal with a broad range of issues. When it comes to caregiving, many support groups are available, and many of these focus on specific topics related to aging, such as these:

Alzheimer's	widowhood
dementia	terminal illness
disabilities and handicaps	hospice care
grief, loss, and mourning	end-of-life decision making

As you process your relationship with your aging parent, other issues may also be adding stress to your life, such as divorce, single parenting, unemployment, finance, health concerns, and depression. Support groups that address these topics are probably meeting in your area. Conduct an online search soon and get connected. Check with area churches, community centers, and nonprofit organizations. Gone are the days when attending a support group was considered weak, when silent shame and guilt accompanied members into each session.

The Common Denominator

Our aging parents' specific issues may vary, but our situations share one common denominator: us. In this we are one—we are all adult children trying to set boundaries, find balance, and stop our own negative behaviors.

There is strength in numbers—we need the help of a support group. AA works because one alcoholic helps another. Support groups for setting boundaries and finding sanity work for the same reason— one adult child in pain helps another as they share resources, stories, techniques, wisdom, and strength.

Nowhere in Scripture is the importance of traveling the road together more beautifully depicted than in Ecclesiastes 4:9-12:

> Two are better than one, because they have a good return for their work: If one falls down, his friend can help him up. But pity the man who falls and has no one to help him up! Also, if two lie down together, they will keep warm. But how can one keep warm alone? Though one may be overpowered, two can defend themselves. A cord of three strands is not quickly broken.

Parents and grandparents who have participated in a 12-week SANITY support group program frequently talk about the unity they feel almost from the beginning. Life-giving fellowship grows as together they work through the companion study guide, completing the weekly assignments and sharing their stories. Each session opens in prayer, and the group recites the SANITY Support Group Network creed.

We need others around us in good times and bad. In times of trial and tribulation, fellow brothers and sisters can lend life-changing support and encouragement by listening, praying, and offering a shoulder to lean on.

Four Kinds of Support Groups

Many kinds of support groups are available, and frankly, the important thing is not *which kind* we join but rather *that* we join. Listening to others share their perspective and their pain helps us be objective—something many of us are not good at. "Letting it all hang out" in a safe and nonjudgmental environment can be both healing and empowering.

Self-help support groups. These are organized and managed by the group members, usually volunteers. Alcoholics Anonymous (AA), Co-Dependents Anonymous (CoDA), Celebrate Recovery, and Six Steps to SANITY support groups are examples of self-help groups. They are also sometimes referred to as fellowships, peer support groups, mutual help groups, or mutual-aid self-help groups.

Professionally run support groups. These are facilitated by professionals, such as a social worker, a psychologist, or a pastor. The facilitator guides discussions and provides other managerial services. Professionally run groups are usually found in institutional settings, such as hospitals, drug-treatment centers, and correctional facilities. They may or may not require a fee for membership.

Online support groups. These have been around since Internet access became readily available. Diverse remote networking formats have allowed the development of synchronous groups, where individuals can exchange messages in real time, as well as asynchronous groups, where members who are not connected to a network at the same time can read and exchange messages. E-mail, Usenet, Internet bulletin boards, chat rooms, and blogs have become popular methods of communication for self-help groups and facilitated support groups.

Support groups have long offered companionship and information for people coping with diseases or disabilities, but online groups have expanded to offer support for people facing specific life circumstances, especially those involving personal and cultural relationships. The wide range of support groups now active on the Internet can offer individuals support for an equally wide range of life circumstances. Finding an online support group is easy, but finding the right one may be difficult. (Six Steps to SANITY support groups are now available online. Visit our website for information at www.settingboundaries.com.)

Six Steps to SANITY support groups. These groups are meeting across the Unites States and many other countries, including New Zealand, South Africa, Canada, Japan, England, and Germany. Using the *Setting Boundaries* book, a companion study guide, and a 12-week audio series, support groups meet in homes, churches, businesses, and community centers. Parents and grandparents are finding hope, healing, and SANITY from the enabling epidemic sweeping our nation. A 12-week support group for parents is now available online, so parents and grandparents can participate from their own homes.

We'll soon be launching a new 12-week program and companion study guide to accompany this book you now hold. To find out where a Six Steps to SANITY support group may be meeting in your neighborhood, or for guidelines how to begin your own, visit our website at www.settingboundaries.com. Since the SANITY Support Group Network launched in 2008, hundreds of parents and grandparents have found hope and healing. I pray the same results will occur as adult children come together to set boundaries with aging parents.

We are in a season of life that will most certainly require every ounce of love and fortitude we can muster. When our strength runs low, we need others who are willing to intervene on our behalf and hold us up. We must learn to look at our circumstances objectively, emotionally distancing ourselves from our situations in order to gain a healthy perspective. Making clear choices based on facts and not on feelings will be critical as we move ahead. The best way to do this is through prayer and group support.

Balancing Actions

1. List support groups you have personally attended.

2. List the support groups you are aware of in your local area, including those being attended by someone you know.

3. List the benefits of attending a support group.

4. Go online and visit www.settingboundaries.com.

14

N—*Nip* Excuses in the Bud

When we make the decision to step out of our role as enabler in our parents' drama, the production can quickly turn into a melodrama. When we decide to set boundaries and find balance, the excuses for our parents' behavior (or our own) can spring up like weeds.

- "Dad made some bad spending choices this past month, but he's promised to do better. I'm just going to help him out a little one more time."

- "He had a really bad childhood, and that's why he..."

- "I asked Mom not to drop by every day to visit, but I feel bad when she..."

- "Dad has had a rough year. He didn't mean to hit Mom—I'm sure it was an accident."

- "Mom never had much when she was a kid, so I can't fault her for wanting a few nice things. She doesn't mean to overspend."

- "I don't have time for Bible study. God understands how busy I am. There's no way He expects me to have a quiet time every day."

One of those excuses has been my nemesis for ages. Can you think of any excuses that frequently pop into your head?

As I travel the country sharing my U-turn testimony from New Age secular humanism to Christianity, I like to say, "I was so open minded my brain slipped out." This comment always brings a wave of laughter from the audience, yet I pray the deeper meaning isn't lost. During my years as an unbeliever, I bought the worldly lie that virtually everything is acceptable—that our responses depend solely on how we personally view situations or on the extenuating circumstances and therefore cannot be judged as right or wrong. There was no overarching standard by which I lived and parented my son. Everything was acceptable, so nothing was sinful. I raised tolerance to an art form.

Of paramount significance was the lack of spiritual consistency in my life and in my son's life. I had a litany of excuses for the ever-changing spiritualities I adopted for a while and then discarded.

But then my life changed—and so did my excuses.

As a new believer, I treasured Bible study and looked forward to it daily. When I first discovered the wisdom contained in the Word, I was hooked. Because my initial hunger for knowledge was so visceral, I assumed spiritual discipline came automatically with salvation. Both were new to me and transformed my life in ways I'd never imagined possible.

But something happened. Over time, I let the busyness of the world slink back into my life and rob me of quiet devotional time, and soon my faith became as flimsy as the excuses I had for no longer making God's Word a priority. Cloud and Townsend speak of the importance of God's Word:

> When some people read the Bible, they see a book of rules, dos and don'ts. When others read it, they see a philosophy of life, principles for the wise. Still others see mythology, stories about the nature of human existence and the human dilemma.

> Certainly, the Bible contains rules, principles, and stories that explain what it is like to exist on this Earth. But to us, the Bible is a living book about relationship. Relationship of God

to people, people to God, and people to each other. It is about the God who created this world, placed people in it, related to people, lost their relationship, and continues to heal that relationship. It is about God as creator: This is his creation. It is about God as a ruler: He ultimately controls his world and will govern it. And it is about God as redeemer: He finds, saves, and heals his loved ones who are lost and in bondage.[1]

Healthy boundaries are tools for healing our broken relationships. To use them effectively, we need to learn new behaviors. We need to learn new standards by which to live. We need to stop making excuses that justify negative behavior and keep us from walking in right priorities. If we want to discover a serene place of balance, we must create opportunities to spend time with the only one who can lead us into a balanced lifestyle—God.

In some seasons in my life, Bible study and devotional reading were the last things I wanted to do. Yet those were the seasons when I needed to make those things even greater priorities. I often learned the hard way—by sacrificing my sanity.

My worn-out excuse, "I don't have time for Bible study—God understands how busy I am," occasionally creeps into my thoughts and words, and when it does, I quickly nip it in the bud. Clearly this is only one excuse we need to identify and reject. But I hear it time and again as I travel the country and talk with stressed-out moms, dads, and adult children. Pray for God to alert you when excuses begin to sprout in your heart so you can eradicate them from your life before they bear their poisonous fruit.

We can also pray that God will help us nip in the bud our excuses for our aging parents' unacceptable behavior—violence, addictions, and other dangerous and potentially life-threatening habits.

As you practice the Six Steps to SANITY, you'll learn to quickly identify excuses in your own life as well as in others'. Once we identify an excuse for what it really is—a way to justify an unhealthy lifestyle and avoid the truth—we can then address the real issue at the heart of the matter.

Balancing Actions

1. Has someone recently said something to you that you immediately knew was an excuse? Write it down.

2. Do you have a consistent excuse for not setting boundaries with your parents? Write it down.

15

I—*Implement* Rules and Boundaries

Implementing rules and boundaries means taking action. We can talk all we want about finding sanity, but until we're willing to do the necessary work to change, very little will change.

You know things have got to change. You've already done a lot of hard work in part one, and now it's time to move forward. Part of change is saying the truth out loud—telling it to ourselves and to others. Cloud and Townsend call this the law of exposure.

The Law of Exposure

A boundary is a property line. It defines where you begin and end. We have been discussing why you need such a line. One reason stands above all the others: You do not exist in a vacuum. You exist in relation to God and others. Your boundaries define you in relation to others.

The whole concept of boundaries has to do with the fact that we exist in relationship. Therefore, boundaries are really about relationship, and finally about love. That's why the Law of Exposure is so important.

The Law of Exposure says that your boundaries need to be made visible to others and communicated to them in relationship. We have many boundary problems because of relational fears. We are beset by fears of guilt, not being liked, loss of love, loss of connection, loss of approval, receiving anger, being known, and so on. These are all failures in love, and God's plan is that we learn how to love. These relational problems can only be solved in relationships, for that is the context of the problems themselves, and the context of spiritual existence.

Because of these fears, we try to have secret boundaries. We withdraw passively and quietly, instead of communicating an honest no to someone we love. We secretly resent instead of telling someone that we are angry about how they have hurt us. Often, we will privately endure the pain of someone's irresponsibility instead of telling them how their behavior affects us and other loved ones, information that would be helpful to their soul.

In other situations, a partner will secretly comply with her spouse, not offering her feelings or opinions for 20 years, and then suddenly "express" her boundaries by filing for divorce. Or parents will "love" their children by giving in over and over for years, not setting limits, and resenting the love they are showing. The children grow up never feeling love, because of the lack of honesty, and their parents are befuddled, thinking, "After all we've done."

In these instances, because of unexpressed boundaries, the relationships suffer. An important thing to remember about boundaries is that they exist, and they will affect us, whether or not we communicate them. We suffer when we do not communicate the reality of our boundaries. If our boundaries are not communicated and exposed directly, they will be communicated indirectly or through manipulation.[1]

One of the best ways to communicate our new boundaries, to "directly expose" them, is to put them in writing. We may be the only people who ever see this document, but we need to develop it nonetheless.

But I'm not a planner, Allison. I'm not a writer. I'm really not very good at things like this.

Is that an excuse I hear? If so, nip it in the bud!

Here's a great way to look at this step. Let's say you have an outdated kitchen. You know it's not working for you, so you decide to do a major remodel. You gather pen and paper and start your list:

1. Problems
   a. Cupboards too small
   b. Dishwasher broken
   c. Not enough counter space

2. Solutions
   a. Replace cupboards and dishwasher
   b. Build a center island

3. Priorities
   a. With five kids, I need my dishwasher!

4. Consequences
   a. An island would take up space.
   b. The cost will eat into savings.
   c. Our family life will be disrupted.
   d. We'll have a kitchen that actually works!

5. Consult professionals
   a. Builders and contactors
   b. Others who have remodeled

6. Test
   a. Show plans to others and solicit feedback.
   b. Make a model.

7. Begin
   a. Complete plans.
   b. Get bids and finalize the budget.
   c. Choose contractor or do it alone.

Get the picture? Your journey to setting healthy boundaries is like a remodel of your life! Implementing rules and boundaries includes many of the same steps:

Identify what isn't working.

Determine a solution.

Prioritize what needs to happen first.

Consider the consequences.

Discuss your plan with a support group.

Rehearse and practice.

Begin.

When adult children share their new boundaries in writing with their aging parents, things begin to happen. They create a new level of open and honest communication. Assumptions and silence no longer cause problems.

It's time for irresponsibility and unaccountability to stop. It's time to "expose" your boundary goals—to yourself and to those you love.

Implementing rules and boundaries requires the important step of exploring expectations and consequences. This is where you decide what you want to accomplish and what the consequences may be when you move toward those goals. The more prepared you are, the more likely you are to maintain your resolve. It's often the surprises that throw us for a loop. We must have a game plan that is thorough and flexible enough to handle unexpected circumstances. To prepare for possible scenarios, write down and rehearse responses to situations that could arise. You probably won't be able to predict everything, but you know your parents, and you most likely know their hot-button topics.

For example, let's say your father criticizes you unkindly or treats you disrespectfully. You don't react emotionally because you are prepared. You respond by saying, "You seem to be having a bad day today; I'll come by another time." Then you smile and leave. No excuses, no apologies—after all, you haven't done anything wrong. If you are on the phone when this occurs, don't hang up rudely or pretend nothing happened. Instead, in a calm and steady voice say, "I'll call back when you're feeling better. Bye." Then hang up.

Your father may be startled at first, and he may even express anger, but don't engage in a debate. Be consistent, and he will eventually alter his behavior toward you. He probably wants your presence in his life. You may not change his basic disposition, but he is likely to be more careful when he is with you. If he doesn't alter his behavior, you already know what to do because you have considered the consequences. Be careful not to raise your voice in anger—you lose power as you increase volume.

Consider another example. Let's say you have decided never to say yes to anything without taking time to think it through (an excellent habit to cultivate, by the way). Your mother calls and wants you to take her to a doctor appointment tomorrow afternoon. You tell her you will look at your calendar and get back to her. You may know perfectly well you have the time and are willing to take her, but you wait a few hours before responding. This does two things: First, it tells her you have a schedule to consider and you cannot be expected to automatically say yes to her every request. Second, it reminds her that your life is separate from hers. If you actually do have something planned tomorrow afternoon, ask if the appointment is urgent. If it isn't, offer to take her another time. If it is urgent, discuss other transportation options.

Will you feel guilty telling her no? Probably, but get over it. You are not rejecting your mother, you are simply honoring your boundary. Will she be upset with you because you won't change your plans? Probably, but she'll get over it too.

This boundary example illustrates a classic one-liner: Stress is what happens when your insides are saying, *I can't do this*, and your mouth is saying, "Of course. I would be happy to."

If we truly want to find balance, we must become strong and take control of the things we *can* control. It's never too late to implement rules and boundaries—to make choices that will change our lives. Trust that God *can* transform your relationship with your parents.

Balancing Actions

1. Describe the process of implementing rules and boundaries.

2. What areas in your life need to be remodeled?

16

T—*Trust* Your Instincts

I'm amazed so many of us make important decisions about life and relationships that are directly opposed to our gut feelings and natural instincts. We know what is right, yet we allow our emotions or excuses to control us.

Dozens of parents in pain who responded to my first questionnaire berated themselves for not paying more attention to their instincts. One anonymous mother had a particularly bad experience:

> My son drove a new car and had two—not one, but two— fancy motorcycles. He had a good job selling office equipment, but I knew he wasn't making enough money to afford those things. He had all kinds of reasons for the stuff he brought home: "A friend gave me this cool MP3 player," or "I got a great deal on the cycle; I couldn't pass it up," or "I'm just storing the 42-inch flat-panel TV here until my buddy moves." On and on the stories went. I was such a sap to believe him, and what makes me even angrier is that I had a feeling something wasn't right. I felt in my gut that something was wrong.

> He was arrested for dealing drugs. When the police searched our home, they found a floor safe under the carpet in his room containing cash, jewelry, cocaine, and methamphetamine. He'd installed a floor safe in our home without our knowledge! It cost us considerable legal fees to clear our own names

because we faced charges of being accessories. Although it was embarrassing to admit that we were duped in such a way, it was more of a nightmare to think we might actually have to suffer the consequences of not following our instincts. Thankfully, we were exonerated, but our son is serving an extended sentence in a federal prison. He has placed our names on the list of visitors he refuses to see.

Did this happen overnight? Did young Johnny wake up one day deciding to deal drugs, using his parent's home as a storehouse for his stash? Highly unlikely. Likewise, did our aging parents only recently begin treating us so poorly? Or have their toxic behaviors been present for years? Have we been ignoring boundaries and accepting excuses for so long that our chaos detectors are broken?

Intuition is a powerful tool. However, if we continue to ignore that inner voice, it will eventually stop talking altogether. We often know in our gut when things are not right—when that inner voice speaks to our heart about specific situations or issues. Yet we repeatedly ignore the voice and negate the instinct.

When I was a girl, I loved to watch the TV program *Lost in Space*. The Robinson family had such amazing adventures. For years afterward, anytime I felt in my gut that trouble was imminent, I would hear the warning phrase of the robot echo in my mind: "Danger, Will Robinson! Danger, Will Robinson!" Oh, that we had our own flailing-armed robot to shout words of warning to us concerning our inability to set appropriate boundaries! As I wrote in my book *Setting Boundaries with Your Adult Children:*

> In my years as a new Christian, I was given a copy of *The Bible Promise Book,* a paperback filled with Scripture listed under alphabetical categories ranging from "Anger" to "Word of God." I've gone through numerous copies of this powerful little paperback over the years, since it leads me to Scripture based on the issues I'm experiencing. Under the topic "Trust" are multiple verses to study, including Proverbs 3:5-6: "Trust in the Lord with all your heart and lean not on your own

understanding; in all your ways acknowledge him, and he will make your paths straight."

If we trust in the Lord with all our heart, we must also trust what he teaches us about the power of the Holy Spirit: "And I will ask the Father, and he will give you another Counselor to be with you forever—the Spirit of truth. The world cannot accept him, because it neither sees him nor knows him. But you know him, for he lives with you and will be in you" (John 14:16-17).

I'm not a theologian, but I know there are countless reference materials available on the amazing power of the Holy Spirit. However, in my experience I've found this one thing to be true: When I am walking in God's will for my life, I can clearly feel the power of the Holy Spirit within me, and this often manifests itself in very distinct impressions of how I should respond, behave, and think. It's as though my "instinct" is a divine power, guiding me to do what is right.

Now, lest you think I have an inside track to discernment, let me assure you this powerful "inside track" guidance is available to each and every one of us who believes. Although I've never heard audible words shouting in my head, "Hey, Allison, don't believe a word he's saying," I have felt distinct impressions over the years that I have both acted upon and ignored. And, without a doubt, the times I ignored that still, small, inner voice, I ended up kicking myself in the backside and saying something akin to this: "I'm so mad at myself! I knew I shouldn't have said such-and-such or done such-and-such. Why didn't I listen to my instincts?"

That's a good question—why don't we? Well, maybe one reason is that we know if we acknowledge it, we must then address it. But if we ignore what our intuition is telling us, we can ignore the issue. Pretend it isn't so. Or perhaps it's just our imagination.[1]

In order to set boundaries and find sanity, we must become willing to embrace changes in our behavior, responses, schedules, motivation, and priorities. This begins with putting God first in our lives, building a relationship with Him, trusting Him. We grow in knowledge and wisdom as we grow in God's Word. The more we know and trust Him, the more we can trust our instincts.

This process of trusting our instincts and not worldly lies, purely emotional responses, or even our head knowledge becomes more natural as we understand God's truth and hide it in our hearts. We need roots that are firmly established in the nurturing soil of life with God. We need to know the standard God has established for us, His children, and the powerful truth contained in His Word. Then, when the still small voice of the Holy Spirit speaks to us, we will hear it more clearly and trust it more implicitly.

Is something telling you not to engage in another argument, but to respond in a new way? Is something telling you to reach out and hug your mother when every fiber of your being wants to turn around and walk away? Can you hear God's Word speaking to your heart, telling you to stop leaning on your own understanding and start trusting Him?

Is that still small voice getting louder? If so, listen to it. Trust your instincts.

Balancing Actions

1. Recall a time when you didn't listen to your instincts and things turned out poorly.

2. List several things you know about the leading of the Holy Spirit.

3. Satan can try to deceive us and speak to our hearts. How do we know whose voice we are hearing?

17

Y—*Yield* Everything to God

Hundreds of people around the country responded to my survey, and nearly all agreed that when we set boundaries with our loved ones, we must yield our situations to God. Yet they also agreed that this is one of the most challenging aspects of living out our faith.

True Growth Requires Letting Go

Leslie Vernick is a licensed clinical social worker and the director of Christ-Centered Counseling for Individuals and Families. Day after day, she witnesses firsthand the devastating effects people's past experiences have on their present lives. In virtually every issue of our lives, many of us make the mistake of clinging tightly to the reigns of our lives or the lives of others. In her book *The Emotionally Destructive Relationship*, Leslie Vernick explains that true growth requires letting go:

> When we attempt to accomplish greater emotional and spiritual work, we usually think about all the things we need to *add* to our lives. We want to read and study the Bible, do meaningful ministry, gain greater emotional stability, better our interpersonal skills, or seek additional wisdom. All these endeavors can be helpful in our maturing process. But I have found in my own life as well as in my counseling practice that deeper and more lasting change usually comes about when we regularly practice letting go rather than doing more.

Recently I was speaking with Richard, a client who feared God's judgment when he died because he wasn't working harder to do more. As we talked I said, "Perhaps we've gotten the concept of final judgment wrong. What if, in the end, Jesus isn't going to tell us everything we've ever done wrong or failed to do? What if he's going to show us the person we could have become and the things we would have done if only we allowed him to heal and mature us?"[1]

True healing begins when we make the head-to-heart connection that we must "let go and let God" in all things, including our painful relationships with our aging parents. Vernick continues:

Letting go in order to grow can be scary. It requires change, which demands a certain degree of faith and hope. That's why our picture of God must heal, at least a little, before we can embark on greater growth.

The writer of Hebrews reminds us that we can only let go and run the race of life well when we keep our eyes on Jesus. Abiding and surrender...continue to be important as we practice the discipline of letting go.

There are three things we must learn to let go of if we want greater healing and maturity in our lives...[2]

Leslie goes on to explain that we must let go of unrealistic expectations, negative emotions, and lies. When we have accomplished the "letting go" part in our hearts and are focused on "letting God," something amazing begins to happen. We feel free. We don't realize how much our fears have imprisoned us until those fears are gone.

You may have heard me talk about my relationship with my adult son—my only child. Sharing parts of the story without tears is still very difficult for me, even after countless interviews and presentations. Some aspects of setting boundaries are painful. Sometimes doing the right thing is painful.

I don't know exactly what you are going through right now concerning your relationship with your parents. I don't know the level of pain, frustration, or defeat you may feel. And I don't have specific answers for how you are going to get to the other side of this chasm that separates you from your parents. But I do know this. I know that until you can yield your situation to God, until you can open your arms wide and release the people you love to Him, any kind of true healing is virtually impossible.

When I had an almost soul-shattering realization that I had been assuming the role of God in my son's life, both of our lives finally began to change. When I was fully able to yield, when I stopped trying to be God in my son's life, he found God.

Christopher turned 38 years old a short time ago. The day brought no celebration—no cake, no gifts, no reminiscing or hugs—because he was in a maximum security prison in Minnesota. I was unable to visit him because I live in Texas and could not make the trip north. We did, however, talk on his birthday. And although I could not see his face or hold him in a motherly embrace, I could nonetheless hear the hope in his voice. His words provided evidence that God is moving in a mighty way in his life.

I knew many years ago that when I established firm boundaries to no longer accept responsibility for his choices, the consequences could be severe. I prepared myself as much as I could. I stopped bailing him out of jail. I stopped allowing him to crash at our home when he was evicted from wherever he had been living. He has lived on the streets, in shelters, in a car, at friends' homes…wherever he could. Eventually he got tired of running from his consequences.

When he turned himself in to the authorities, I clung to the knowledge that even though he would spend years behind bars, God had a plan for my son. I fought feelings of guilt, refusing to let Satan win. I held firm to the conviction that my son was in prison not because I set boundaries, but because of his own choices and actions.

When I stepped out of the way and yielded Chris to God, he began the journey he was destined to walk—a journey I had often delayed because I thought I was helping, because I couldn't nip excuses in the bud, didn't trust my instincts, and wouldn't consistently implement rules and boundaries.

Over the past several years, I have watched from afar as God has

"The Lord disciplines those he loves, and he punishes everyone he accepts as a son." Endure hardship as discipline; God is treating you as sons. For what son is not disciplined by his father?

HEBREWS 12:6-7

disciplined my son—His son. I've watched this angry, irresponsible, and fatherless boy become a man who loves the Lord as an obedient son. I've watched as trials and tribulations have tested his faith. Even while he is in prison, he is experiencing a new freedom in Christ.

In a recent letter, he shared a poem that the Lord placed on his heart. I am including it exactly as he sent it—without edits.

Now

It does not matter who you are,
yor age, race, or if your parents loved you or not.
Let that go, it belongs in the past, you belong to the now.
It does not matter what you have been
the things you did wrong, the many mistakes we did,
all the people we have hurt.
We must learn to forgive ourselves, accept ourselves, love ourselves,
let the past belong to the past.
love the lord and feel the holy spirit run threw us,
trully know and submit to the realization
the lord has forgiven us of our sins.
celebrate your self now begin now
begin to love yourself
start anew
give yourself a new birth today
today can be a new beginning of a new you and a new life...

CJ SMITH

A new you and a new life—the tangible result of finding sanity.

Yielding everything to God does not mean giving up. It is not a sign of defeat or weakness; in fact, it's quite the opposite. The more I yielded, the more clarity I had in my life, and the more freely my son was able to walk on his own path of destiny—a path that has led to more healing than I could have imagined.

Today, my son and I are working together to define and document the critical steps we must take to restore a relationship that has been ravaged by poor choices, addictions, incarceration, and estrangement. What does forgiveness really look like? How do we learn to trust again? How can families heal and build new memories after setting healthy (and sometimes very painful) boundaries?

> Come near to God and he will come near to you.
>
> JAMES 4:8

We have a great many questions that we are looking to God to answer, questions we would not be asking had we not yielded everything to God first.

We cannot know God's ultimate plan when we fully yield our loved ones to Him. Yet neither we nor our loved ones travel this path alone.

We cannot force God's plan for our lives into a timetable, but we can decide to start making the changes necessary for our hearts and homes to be restored to peace. Will we start now—today? Or will we continue to operate with business as usual?

Are we ready to implement these Six Steps to SANITY and enjoy new beginnings? The choice is ours.

Balancing Actions

1. If God's grace is sufficient, why is yielding to God so difficult?

2. What will have to happen before you are willing to trust that God has things under control?

3. What is the best thing that can happen when you yield your loved ones to God?

Part Three

The Dawn of a New Beginning

There we have them, the Six Steps to SANITY.

> *S*—Stop your own negative behavior (especially stop the flow of money!).
>
> *A*—Assemble a support group.
>
> *N*—Nip excuses in the bud.
>
> *I*—Implement rules and boundaries.
>
> *T*—Trust your instincts.
>
> *Y*—Yield everything to God (let go and let God).

You may feel as though you've been squeezed through a wringer of emotions and have done a lot of soul-searching since chapter 1. My prayer is that even if the road is still rocky, you feel spiritually stronger than ever before and are ready for change.

But you still have work to do. The time has come to develop the written plan that will help you implement these crucial steps and remain focused and on track.

As you begin these steps, the key is to remain cool, calm, collected, and in control during this vital stage of your growth. Don't jump in and declare to our parents, "Enough is enough! That's it! I'm not going to take this anymore!" Try not to make any decisions when you are emotionally stressed. Train yourself to respond rationally and not to react emotionally. When you respond rationally, you are in control. When you react emotionally, others are in control, and you have lost your power. Your parents are more likely to take you seriously if you respond rationally. (This is especially true if they are toxic.) You are free to choose how you will respond to whatever they say or do.

Never underestimate the power of putting your plans and goals in writing. As I've said before, you should do this if for no other reason than to hold yourself accountable for the journey you are about to take. Remember the example of remodeling your kitchen? You wouldn't undergo a project like that without a written plan.

People often begin serious weight-loss programs by creating a written plan. They write down their current weight, measurements, and nutrition habits; some future dietary guidelines, menu plans, and recipes; and their weight-loss goals. Or let's say you are planning a special event at your home. You will probably use more than a few written plans as you prepare, such as shopping lists, guest lists, and a to-do list of tasks to accomplish. These plans help you put together a successful event and keep you from getting stressed. Why, then, do we approach more important issues in our lives with so little planning and forethought?

> A number of years ago I had a career as a professional fundraising executive, and a significant part of my job was to assist board members and nonprofit organizations in the development and implementation of detailed strategic plans. I frequently conducted board retreats and planning workshops to troubleshoot and identify dysfunction within organizations, helping groups and individuals to establish detailed plans to better equip their organization to succeed. Today, my strategic planning workshops are still said to be some of the best available in equipping writers, speakers, and small business owners to succeed.

> Over the years, I tried to implement some of these techniques

with respect to "helping" my son. I would frequently help him to develop life plans and to-do lists to get his life on track—even going so far as to making lists for him myself. As if that was ever going to help him! I now see that my need to keep him on track was just that—*my* need. He had no ownership of the plan, no ownership of the to-do lists. During the times I encouraged him to develop his own to-do lists (more like forced him under duress of grounding or some other punitive punishment) the consequences were either nonexistent, too severe, or had no teeth.

I was unable to see how my desire to help him succeed was actually crippling him. Moreover, for a long time I was unable to see clearly how my own personal issues were contributing causes for the turmoil within our household. I needed direction, healing, and hope—but instead for years I filled the empty places in my heart and soul with everything but those things. It was far less painful to focus on my son and what he needed to do with his life than it was for me to point the spotlight on my own life.[1]

I am a former enabler who has discovered the freedom of setting boundaries and finding sanity. With my newfound perspective, I can see a better way to make plans that will help us stop the insanity and find balance. It's called holding ourselves accountable. But before we take this crucial step, let's review some of what we've covered so far.

How We Arrived at Burnout

1. We neglected to put God at the center of our lives.
2. We lost sight of our priorities.
3. We confused helping with enabling.
4. We confused respect and honor with accepting negative behavior.
5. We didn't understand the value of self-respect.
6. We allowed our own destructive patterns to get in the way.

7. We didn't set clear boundaries.

8. We made emotional choices.

9. We weren't sure what a healthy boundary really was.

10. We felt powerless and out of control.

11. We didn't think we had a choice.

12. We didn't understand about stress and burnout.

That's quite a list, but don't let it overwhelm you! Now that we know how we got here, how can we stop?

How to Stop Repeating Negative Behavior

1. Stop reacting emotionally.

2. Step back.

3. Change priorities.

4. Hand everything over to God.

5. Understand that *you* need to change.

6. Get help for yourself.

7. Value your self-respect.

8. Follow the Six Steps to SANITY.

9. Take responsibility for your own choices.

10. Take time to be alone and reflect, pray, and read the Bible.

11. Focus on what it means to love and be loved.

12. Trust that God is in control and He will make a way.

Remember, the *S* in SANITY is *Stop*. We're on a roll—let's continue...

What We Need to Know to Achieve Balance

1. God has standards for our lives.

2. Boundaries are necessary.

3. Change begins with our own choices.

4. We must determine what motivates us.

5. We must learn how our past is affecting our present.

6. There will be consequences, and some may be painful.

7. We are not alone.

8. It won't always be easy.

9. Love and forgiveness have nearly unlimited power.

10. Each personality type responds to life in a unique way.

11. The Six Steps to SANITY provide a path for us to follow.

12. God loves us and has a plan for us.

Now we're ready for the big kahuna…

How to Find Sanity

1. Nurture a relationship with God.

2. Reprioritize your life.

3. Make a commitment to change.

4. Set healthy boundaries and expose them.

5. Find self-respect.

6. Love and honor your aging parents.

7. Attend support group meetings.

8. Read, research, and acquire knowledge and wisdom.

9. Develop a written plan.

10. Be consistent and always follow through.

11. Apply the Six Steps to SANITY in all areas of life.

12. Speak the truth in love.

I wish I could say, "Well, that's it! Go forth, brothers and sisters, and set boundaries!" I have no doubt you are fully capable of doing just that, but we need to add a few more vital pieces to the puzzle before we have the full picture in view. But we're nearing the homestretch. Grab your notebook and let's get started!

18

Put It in Writing

You've been putting things in writing since you began this book. As we near the end of our journey together, I pray that your notes will consistently lead you back to one solid truth: The Lord will take care of us during this turbulent time (and always)!

Rest assured, God has sustained you and will continue to sustain you.

Your journey in setting boundaries has come to the place where purpose, priorities, plans, and prayer come together to bring you to a place of freedom and help you find sanity.

Tyranny of the Urgent is a classic little book by Charles E. Hummel that was first published in 1967. It's about purpose, priorities, plans, and prayer, and its premise is that we must plan life around priorities or we will be zapped putting out fires all day long. This is a guide to time management in a Christian and biblical context, where God's will and Word take precedence in determining what is important. This important work affirms what I have been saying for years—plans let us stay flexible. A written plan of action affords greater freedom, not bondage.

> Cast your cares on the LORD and he will sustain you; he will never let the righteous fall.
>
> **PSALM 55:22**

The Importance of a Written Plan

In one of the most successful sessions in the Six Steps to SANITY and 12 Weeks to Freedom programs, participants develop a written action plan. Developing a written plan isn't a new idea. It's a necessity that has long been recognized by professional counselors who deal with people in pain every day.

Remember the law of exposure that Cloud and Townsend discussed? It's time to express your boundaries—to expose your expectations. It's time to make commitments and consider the consequences. In short, it's time to be utterly truthful with yourself.

The following chapters include important writing exercises. By the time you reach the end of the book, you'll have a written plan and be ready to respond rationally to your parents the next time a stress trigger flips your switch.

Four Components to Your Written Plan

1. Identify your stress triggers.

2. Define your expectations.

3. Consider the consequences.

4. Prepare for sowing and reaping.

A written action plan guarantees that the newly established rules and boundaries have no gray areas. When we are communicating with our aging parents, this step is primarily *for our own benefit*. Your parents don't necessarily need to see your written plan. You are not trying to teach them, as if they were your children. Rather, you are communicating to your parents with respect and honor. You are unveiling your new boundaries and explaining how you would like your parents to respect these boundaries even though they may not always agree with them.

My prayer is that you will be empowered to move forward with this crucial step. May you regain hope and healing in your home, and may the bond of love and respect in your heart be strengthened. If you've reached the place where you *know* change has to happen, con-gratulations—the hard work has already been accomplished. Many people never reach this stage and instead continue for years and years through crisis after crisis. They never make a commitment to establish a written plan of action to change.

Balancing Actions

1. How do you feel about putting your plans to set bound-aries in writing?
2. Explain why this is an important step.

Here are some ways you can prepare to write your Plan of Action.

- Conduct a thorough self-examination of your role in the situation.
- Consult with a professional regarding personal issues.
- Connect with a support group.
- Agree with your spouse on your course of action.
- Compile and review your written notes.
- Emotionally distance yourself from the situation and make an objective assessment.
- Role-play with yourself, verbally exposing your new boundary.
- Carefully review all Six Steps to SANITY.
- Pray and then pray again. Then pray some more.

19

Stress Triggers

What do you want to change? What boundary do you need to establish and clarify? What is causing you pain? What is hurting your heart? Get your notebook and write this at the top of a clean page:

> Trigger points—things that stress me out about my aging parents:

Now start writing.

Your Written Plan—Step One: Identify Your Stress Triggers

Remember, your parents won't be seeing this list—it's only for you, your spouse, and perhaps your support group. You may decide after reviewing your list that some of your issues aren't really issues at all. That's okay—you will prioritize your list later. For now, just let your pen fly. Write down every possible item you can think of.

Here's a list from one of my questionnaire respondents. It's pretty clear that Lisa has a somewhat toxic dad and that she has never set clear and firm boundaries with him. Notice also that some items may sound trivial to you. But remember that we all have different personality types, so something that doesn't seem important to you might be very important to someone else. This is a key principle to remember in all relationships: We must respect each other's differences.

Things That Stress Me Out About My Dad
—My Trigger Points

1. It drives me nuts when Dad walks into my house and opens the refrigerator or cupboards and helps himself to food without asking or being invited—as though he lives here. I don't mind feeding him, and what I have is his, but that's not the point.

2. I feel used when Dad and I are getting gas at a convenience store or grocery shopping and he asks me to pick up a pack of cigarettes for him and tells me he'll pay me back later. He never does, and cigarettes are expensive! My husband and I don't smoke, and we have a budget we're doing our best to follow. This is beginning to get out of hand.

3. Dad has been bringing a six-pack of beer to the house on Sunday evenings when he comes for dinner and drinks it all within a couple of hours. Jessica asked me why Grandpa "talks funny" after he drinks his "brew." My six-year-old is seeing her grandfather get drunk in front of her and refers to beer as *brew*! Who told her that? Dad says it's "only beer" and not hard liquor or anything.

4. My dad borrows tools from Scott and sometimes just helps himself to things in our garage, and it takes forever to get them back. And when we do, they are often dirty, damaged, and not in the condition they were in when he borrowed them. He doesn't respect us or our stuff.

5. It hurts me when Dad says cruel things about my mom. She moved out of state and remarried after they got divorced three years ago. He's very bitter, and maybe he has reason to be, but I don't want to hear about their personal issues, and I don't want to hear him talk dirt about her…especially not in front of my kids.

6. Dad just turned 72, and I'm worried that if he doesn't start taking better care of himself, I'm going to end up having to take care of him, and I don't want to. I love my dad, he's my dad, but he's a mean, stubborn man who makes everyone around him miserable. If he came to live with us, I could see him alienating my kids and driving off my husband, and then it would be the two of us until one of us dies. That's not how I envision my life.

This is only a sampling of the list Lisa sent—it was quite lengthy. I could tell she was really venting her frustration. The further she developed her list, the more telling her notes became, as though every item she wrote gave her more strength to identify and address the things that were actually causing her the most pain.

This is a good exercise for all of us to do at this stage. Make your list as long (or short) as needed. No holds barred. There is no right or wrong.

Please don't underestimate the power of this step.

After you've completed this exercise, review your list with your spouse and support group members. Pray about it. When you are ready, select your top three stress triggers. Number them from one (the most harmful to your heart) to three.

Before we move on to our next chapter, I'd like to address one more thing. If you are married, I hope you've been talking with your spouse about setting boundaries. If not, the time has come to do that. As you have learned, our second-highest priority (after our relationship with God) is our relationship with our spouse.

If you are experiencing boundary issues in your marriage as well as with your parents (which, by the way, isn't unusual), I encourage you to utilize the same Six Steps to SANITY to give you the strength you need to communicate effectively with your spouse. This is a critical priority and needs to be addressed *before* you begin to make significant changes in your relationship with your aging parents. Please seek the help of a reliable counselor or perhaps a pastor if your marriage is in any way suffering from weak boundaries. Don't wait another day.

Balancing Actions

1. What is the main point of this chapter?

2. Are you stronger today than when you first began reading this book? In what ways?

3. How did you feel when you started writing down all your stress triggers? When you finished?

4. Do you think you were honest in developing your list?

5. What are your top three stress triggers?

20

Expectations

Your expectations are the goals you hope to achieve as you set bound-aries. Several of the balancing actions have prompted you to clarify what you hope to achieve on this journey. Review your notes from past chapters—refresh your mind—and thank God for your ability to make new choices and changes. Continue to pray that He will renew your mind and give you wisdom so you can make the right decisions.

In order to define your expectations, review your stress-trigger list and ask yourself these two questions:

> *What do I really want?*
>
> *What do I hope to gain?*

This isn't the time for noncommittal responses like these: "Gosh, I think it might be nice if my mom wouldn't just drop by whenever she wants," or "Um...I...well, maybe my mom could call first before coming over."

Do you really want to set boundaries and find balance? Do you want to retrieve the self-respect you have lost? Do you want to be taken seriously? If you do, tell yourself what you want and what you hope to gain. This is not selfish or self-centered—it's smart. Make a com-mitment so you can set a boundary. Start writing.

Your Written Plan—Step Two: Define Your Expectations

Use your stress-trigger list to decide what you ultimately want to achieve by setting boundaries. Expectations can look like this:

> I want my mom to stop dropping by the house without calling.
>
> I want my dad to stop swearing around my children.
>
> I want my parents to stop asking for money when they gamble theirs away.
>
> I want my mom to stop bringing gifts for the children every time she visits.
>
> I want Dad to stop being verbally judgmental about our faith.

After prayerful review and discussion with her husband, Lisa decided these were her top three stress triggers:

1. drinking beer in our home
2. asking me to buy him cigarettes
3. taking food or using things without asking

These were Lisa's expectations:

1. I want my dad to be sober when he is in our home.
2. I want to stop supporting my father's nicotine addiction.
3. I want Dad to respect our property when he comes to our home.

Do you see how she has prioritized and fine-tuned steps one and two from her original list of trigger points?

Once again, discuss your list with your spouse and your support group. We do not live in a vacuum. Remember that God created us to be in relationship, and besides, the journey you are on can be challenging at times. We all need the love and support of others who respect us and can help us to be strong.

To achieve your goals—your expectations—you will eventually have to take action. Writing down your expectations and praying about them is a good start, but you should not expect God to make them all come to pass without further cooperation from you. That's not how it works. So in chapter 21, let's take the next big step and look at some consequences.

Balancing Actions

1. Was it difficult to write down what you wanted? Why or why not?

2. How did you decide which stress triggers to choose as the top three priorities?

21

Consequences

As you begin to set healthy boundaries, two things are very likely to happen. Your loved ones may experience painful realities, and you may encounter outside resistance. Some people will fight hard against your new limits, so let's make sure you're ready to respond appropriately. If you do, others are more likely to eventually accept and respect your new boundaries. Your mother may finally learn that she can no longer have it her way all the time and that she needs to consider other people's needs as well as her own. Your father may come to understand that you are not rejecting him when you refuse to loan money.

Your Boundaries and Others' Pain

You may feel uncomfortable making changes that could bring consequences to other people's lives. Yet significant change almost always includes some pain both for ourselves and for those around us. That's why we need to prepare ourselves by including an extensive list of possible consequences in our written plan. Consider every possible scenario you can imagine. Some might actually happen and some might not, but you'll be prepared to respond effectively if they do.

Here are four things you can do to make this step work for you:

1. Overcome your fear of consequences.

2. Expect some consequences will occur and be willing to live with them.

3. Prepare for as many possible consequences as you can—positive and negative.

4. Focus on the consequences for you, not the consequences for your parents.

In her book *Parents, Teens, and Boundaries,* Dr. Jane Bluestein makes a good point:

> In the process of establishing healthy belief systems and behaviors, our progress can be seriously set back by the negative reactions of others, especially if we have a history of people-pleasing. If most of our friends and family members are used to seeing us as care-takers, people with no clear sense of boundaries, people who consistently place higher priorities on other people's needs than our own, they will certainly respond in whatever way seems necessary to maintain status quo. One woman lamented, "I've tried setting boundaries, but my parents get hurt, my husband gets mad, and my kids feel abandoned. What's the use?"
>
> What's the use, indeed? People do what works, and our loved ones can become fairly aggressive when old tactics fail them. By the same token, we can take drastic measures when our self-protection becomes important enough.[1]

You've already decided it's time to take action—that's why you're reading this book and completing the balancing actions at the end of every chapter. Considering the consequences may be one of the most difficult steps to complete. Change often comes at a price, so we need to determine whether we are willing and able to afford it.

David Hawkins encourages us to consider some of the consequences of change:

Changing our circumstances changes us.

When we change, those around us often change as well.

When we change, we open up possibilities in our lives.

Change inevitably creates anxiety.

Change ultimately brings confidence.[2]

Cloud and Townsend concur:

> Consequences give some good "barbs" to fences. They let people know the seriousness of the trespass and the seriousness of our respect for ourselves. This teaches them that our commitment to living according to helpful values is something we hold dear and will fight to protect and guard.[3]

It may be time for you to fight for your life, for your family, and for your self-respect. Are you ready? Hawkins adds:

> If I have learned one thing about change, it is this: Change does not happen in one fell swoop. It is the result of numerous small steps, many of which you have already begun taking. Change is also not linear. If you look back over your life, you will see the jagged, seesaw path of change. A seed of restlessness led you to become more frustrated and perhaps even angry. Now you are ready to take bigger steps to transform your life.

> You have counted the cost of change. Perhaps it includes summoning the courage to leave a control freak or insist that the aggressor go in for anger management. Or perhaps it includes learning to end the triangulation your mother or father have created in your family. Perhaps you have an image of what you'd like to see changed, and now you are considering the consequences of embarking on this journey.[4]

Whatever the reason, you have decided enough is enough. As we consider the consequences, let's look again at some of the things we fear. We discussed these earlier in chapter 5. What are we afraid of?

loss of love or abandonment

others' anger

feeling lonely

losing the "good me" inside

feeling guilty

Most of all, we are afraid of losing our parents' love when we stand up to them.

Worst-Case Scenarios

In his book *Healing from Family Rifts*, Mark Sichel addresses one of the most painful potential consequences of setting boundaries with our aging parents—being cut off and utterly rejected.

> Grace had always been daddy's girl and mom's mommy. After her parents' divorce, Grace accompanied her dad to social events and was his best pal. Her mom, on the other hand, wallowed in depression and drug abuse for years after the divorce. Grace cleaned the house, cooked, and tried to be her mom's therapist and best friend. Grace came to therapy to work on developing her career as a singer and actress in musical theater. She also worked out her poor choices of men and ended up marrying Rod, a successful restaurateur. Not surprisingly, along the way she also became an independent adult, and stopped the dysfunctional behavior that kept her tied to her parents.
>
> Grace stopped being the caregiver for her mom, and instead gave her the name of a therapist. She began to relate to her dad in more age-appropriate daughterly ways rather than as a companion and a spouse substitute. Then, after she announced her engagement to Rod, both parents stopped speaking to her. Grace was shattered. She was shocked to realize that neither of her parents wanted to have connections and lives of their own and that they resented and envied Grace's new life.[5]

This was no doubt painful for Grace. However, she had the choice to return to her old behaviors and choices—to retain the status quo if she so desired. She decided her impending marriage and self-respect were her new priorities. She made a choice to shift her priorities to the standard set by her adoptive Father—God.

This severing of ties is an unfortunate potential consequence of setting boundaries. Dr. Laura addresses this often.

> When people, even someone you call Mommy or Daddy, will not take responsibility for their dangerous and destructive behaviors, don't seem to have sensitivity to or guilt for the havoc they wreak, and therefore refuse to take steps to improve the situation, you need to start thinking seriously about some degree of disconnect.[6]

Your disconnect from your aging parents may last a few hours, a few days, or a few weeks. It may last even longer. If you set your boundaries consistently, respectfully, and in love, and if you follow through with the stated consequences, your parents will eventually understand that you are serious. If they don't, you must be prepared for that consequence as well.

As we prepare ourselves for change by considering the consequences, we should face the fact that other people are likely to get angry. This is the most common form of resistance we can expect from them. Cloud and Townsend don't pull any punches: "People who get angry at others for setting boundaries have a character problem."[7]

> Though I walk in the midst of trouble, you preserve my life; you stretch out your hand against the anger of my foes, with your right hand you save me.
>
> PSALM 138:7

If your parents have this character problem, the more prepared you are to respond with firmness and love, the better. Nothing will change if you don't. Are you willing to settle for the status quo and continue heading toward burnout? Or, with God's help, are you ready to move toward a life that is pleasing to Him and that will bring you balance and self-respect?

The choice is yours.

However, let's not focus only on the possible negative consequences. Why not consider the likelihood of positive consequences as well? God has given us many promises to help us in time of trouble.

Our parents' responses to our new choices may surprise us—especially when we're utterly truthful and consistently expressing our needs with conviction and love.

Your Written Plan—Step Three: Consider the Consequences

The more detailed and thorough you can get listing the potential consequences, the better. Your goal is to prepare yourself for any possible curveball that may come your way. Therefore, I recommend you make *two* lists:

> List One: A list of your parents' *possible reactions*—
> positive and negative
>
> List Two: A list of your *rational responses* if your parents
> disrespect your new boundary

Get your notebook once again and start writing. You will use the top three stress triggers and the expectations you identified in the previous chapter.

What Might Happen?—Possible Reactions

This is the first of your two lists. What could possibly happen to you and to your aging parents? Include both positive and negative columns. For example, in the negative column you might write, "When I stop making Dad's car payment, he may lose the car, get angry with me, and never want to see me again." "If I tell Mom she can't drop by without calling, she might accuse me of not loving her." "If I insist that my parents move from our home into an assisted-living center, I may be ostracized from my church because they won't understand."

In the positive column, you could list things associated with each of the same items. "We may have enough money to repair the roof of the garage now that we aren't paying for another vehicle." "My mother may begin to make friends with people at the senior center." "My marriage may take a turn for the better as we focus on taking care of ourselves and our marriage and find a less judgmental church home."

What Will You Do?—Rational Responses

This second list is critical and could be far more difficult to develop. You must decide on the definitive boundary-breaking consequences you are prepared to establish. These consequences are the nonnegotiables you develop after prayer, discussion, deliberation, and 100 percent commitment. They are the rational actions you will take if your parents react emotionally. You could write, "If you do not make the next payment on your car as you initially promised you would, we will pick it up and sell it immediately, and you will have to make other transportation arrangements." "If you do not contribute the amount you agreed to contribute on time, you will have to move out in a month." "The next time you disrespect us with profanity, shouting, or verbal abuse of any kind, you will no longer be welcome to live in our home. There is an assisted-living center nearby, and we will move you there within a week."

Lisa was very serious about developing her two lists of consequences. Once she and her husband identified the stress trigger of her father's drinking in their home and determined an appropriate boundary, they were able to consider how he might react and what their response would be.

Possible reactions. If I tell Dad he cannot drink in our home, he could...

> drink before he comes to visit
>
> stop visiting altogether
>
> get angry and storm out
>
> go on a binge and do something drastic
>
> hide alcohol when he visits

bring it anyway and test me to see what I'll do

accept our wishes and comply with them

join a program that will help him stop drinking

My rational responses. If Dad comes to our home drunk or tries to bring beer inside with him…

- If he is drunk, we will not permit him to come inside our home.

- If he tries to bring beer inside with him, I will tell him he can put it in the pantry until he leaves but may not open it in our home.

- If he disrespects that, we will ask him to leave immediately and see him to the door or call the authorities if necessary.

This list must be very specific. Remember, the items on it are not up for debate or negotiation. In order to be effective, the consequences will need to be serious, so you must be certain you have prayerfully considered the options and are willing to follow through. Do not say, "I will call the police if you threaten me" unless you are willing to do so. Do not say, "If you don't make the next payment on the car on time, I will come get it and sell it" unless you are fully prepared to do just that and have a legal right to do it. Don't be like the boy who cried wolf. Cloud and Townsend conclude:

> I have told you these things, so that in me you may have peace. In this world you will have trouble. But take heart! I have overcome the world.
>
> JOHN 16:33

> Behaviors have consequences. As Paul says, "A man reaps what he sows" (Galatians 6:7-8). If we study, we will reap good grades. If we work, we will get a paycheck. If we exercise, we will be in better health. If we act lovingly towards

others, we will have closer relationships. On the negative side, if we sow idleness, irresponsibility, or out-of-control behavior, we can expect to reap poverty, failure, and the effects of loose living. These are natural consequences of our behavior.[8]

> Change almost always comes at a cost. We have to know whether we are willing and able to pay the price.

Boundary-deficient lives subvert the helpful process of natural consequences. Gaining balance will take time—it won't happen overnight—but a positive outcome is possible. Developing these two lists of consequences is vital, and sticking with them is crucial.

Balancing Actions

1. Considering the consequences of setting boundaries is vital. Why?

2. What was the most difficult aspect of this exercise for you?

3. How is God speaking to your heart as you move toward confronting your aging parent with these new boundaries?

Sowing and Reaping

When I was growing up, my Cleveland neighborhood was called a melting pot. Today, it would be called culturally and ethnically diverse. We were white, black, Catholic, Protestant, and Jewish. We were German, Polish, Greek, and Czech. We were very young and very (very) old. Most of us were rich in experience and poor in finances (I lived in the projects), although I suspected the woman who took our money every week at the church where Mom bought fresh handmade pierogi was rich because her earrings always matched the pin she wore. She smiled and called me Bubeleh.

We didn't have a church family—we had a community family. In this family I picked up bits and pieces of wisdom that seeped into my vocabulary (and into my heart and mind as well). I didn't know at the time that many of these tidbits were Bible verses.

I seemed to hear the Golden Rule everywhere. I also heard Galatians 6:7 a lot (long before I knew its origin), usually in this context: "Young lady! You're going to reap what you sow if you don't stop that this instant!" The word *that* could have referred to any number of mischievous things, as I was a very precocious, inquisitive, and dramatic child.

In time, I discovered that Galatians 6:7-11 is one of the most helpful principles in the Bible:

> Do not be deceived: God cannot be mocked. A man reaps what he sows. The one who sows to please his sinful nature, from that nature will reap destruction; the one who sows to please the Spirit, from the Spirit will reap eternal life. Let us not become weary in doing good, for at the proper time we will reap a harvest if we do not give up. Therefore, as we have opportunity, let us do good to all people, especially to those who belong to the family of believers.

When we hear this Scripture, we tend to immediately think of it as a warning against sowing bad seed. Yet its context shows that it's not just about sin and its consequences. It's actually teaching us to choose well and to persevere. When we do, our labor will bear good fruit, and we will succeed at the proper time. Sow good seed, do not become weary or give up, and do good to all people. Amen!

We've come a long way toward avoiding burnout and building mutual respect, and we're in the homestretch now. Let's remind ourselves of the big picture and then zoom in to see where we are: Our goal is to attain sanity, which includes implementing rules and boundaries (the *I* in SANITY). We're creating a written plan that will help us do that, and we've already accomplished three of the four steps in creating this written plan:

Step one: Identify your stress triggers.

Step two: Define your expectations.

Step three: Consider the consequences.

Now let's move on…

Your Written Plan—Step Four: Prepare to Sow and Reap

To set healthy boundaries, you must learn how to say no with conviction and love. This will help you to be an authentic child of God—one who loves truthfully and with respect.

We want to love, honor, and respect our aging parents. We want to do good. But we have discovered that weak boundaries keep us from loving, honoring, and respecting our parents. We have not been doing good to those we love—our parents or ourselves. The time has come to approach our aging parents and tell them how we feel. Are you ready?

Growth in setting boundaries—especially emotional boundaries—must always be at a rate that takes into account your past injuries, the progress you have made to better understand yourself and your family of origin, your commitment to consequences, your willingness to change, and your ability to consistently follow through. If you try to do too much too soon without laying a solid foundation, your entire project could suffer a massive collapse. Cloud and Townsend offer an example of someone whose foundation was less than solid.

> "This boundary teaching doesn't work," complained Frank in a therapy session.
>
> "Why not?" I asked.
>
> "Well, as soon as I understood that I don't set good limits with people, I called my father the same day and gave him what for. Can you believe what he did? He hung up on me! This is great, just great. Boundaries have made things worse for me, instead of better."
>
> Frank is like the over eager child who is too impatient for training wheels on his new bicycle. It's only several falls and skinned knees later that he begins to entertain the possibility that he skipped some steps in his training.
>
> Here is an idea to help you navigate this step. Ask your support group or your friends if you could work on boundaries with them. They will show you their true value in their response to your truth telling. Either they'll warmly cheer you on in being able to disagree with and confront them, or they'll resist you. Either way, you'll learn something. A good supportive relationship cherishes the no of all parties involved. The members know that true intimacy is only built around the freedom to disagree: "He who conceals his hatred has lying lips" (Proverbs 10:18). Begin practicing your no with people who will honor it and love you for it.[1]

Are you ready to start practicing your no? If so, it's time to prepare yourself for what you are going to say and how you are going to say it the next time you are faced with one of your top three stress triggers. Remember, your goal is to respond rationally and not react emotionally. You want to stay in control.

When you feel ready to begin exposing your new boundaries, you have two choices.

Your first option is to wait until your parents pull one of your stress triggers. In this scenario, you immediately stop what is happening and hold your parents accountable, using a prepared script. Remember Cloud and Townsend's Law of Exposure: You need to lovingly communicate with others about their negative behavior and your boundaries.

Your second option is to address your issues with your parents before they pull one of your stress triggers. Perhaps they don't live nearby, and you want to start the process while they are visiting. Or perhaps you want to prevent a stress trigger from happening at an upcoming event. Or perhaps your stress trigger involves a caregiving issue that needs to be addressed in a timely manner.

Regardless of which option you choose, your goal remains the same. In love, and without anger or accusations, identify the behavior and explain why it is no longer acceptable. Do not raise your voice—stay as calm as possible. This is not the time to point fingers, blame, debate, or negotiate. You have reached this decision after a lot of hard work, prayer, and practice. Trust that God will continue to guide your steps as you guard your heart.

Before actually confronting your parents, rehearse your speech with your spouse and your support group. When you meet with your parents, you can either memorize your explanation and your responses to their possible reactions, or you can use notes. Just remember, your notes are for you, not for them.

Each time you set a boundary, use the basic six-step format that follows. Eventually, this will become a habit as you learn how to protect yourself with healthy boundaries and your loved ones begin to understand you are serious when you say no.

A Six-Step Boundary Script

1. *Give assurance.* Convey your boundary in love. Do not react emotionally. Assure your aging parents that you are not rejecting them.

2. *Address the stress trigger.* Expose the negative behavior and the way it makes you feel.

3. *Address why this behavior is unacceptable.* Avoid lengthy reasons or excuses. Be concise.

4. *Clearly state your expectations or goals.* Explain what you expect to start happening immediately.

5. *Identify the consequences.* Clearly state what *will* happen if the negative behavior continues.

6. *Give more assurance.* Once again, convey your boundary in love. Assure your aging parents that you are not rejecting them; you are setting boundaries that will create a better relationship with them.

Here's an example of what these six steps might look like in practice: (the numbers relate to the six-step script above)

> (1) Mom and Dad, we're sorry that we have allowed this to continue for so long, but we've finally decided to make some changes. We love you both, and we want our relationship to be strong and healthy. (2) Watching you yell and fight is not healthy for us or for the children. Your arguments upset everyone, and (3) they show the kids that disrespecting your loved ones is okay. (4) You can choose to disrespect one another in your own home, but not in ours.
>
> What just happened is unacceptable behavior in our home from now on. (5) If it happens again, we will have to ask you

to leave. (6) We love you, but this is a new rule in our home, and we are committed to keeping it.

Let's see how this works for Lisa. Notice how she uses all six steps in her script. Here's the scene: Lisa's dad shows up for Sunday dinner with a six-pack of beer. She greets him at the door when he arrives. Her husband is at work, but they have agreed that Lisa can handle this on her own. She is prepared with their letter in hand. She has practiced by reading this letter out loud to Scott several times, and her voice is clear and sure. She has worked hard not to sound angry, to assure her dad that she loves him, and to be clear that she is very serious about this decision. Here's her script:

> Dad, I need to talk to you about something very serious. I want to make sure I say this right so I'm going to read you something Scott and I wrote.
>
> Dad, Scott and I have talked this over, and we love you very much. But we don't love something you have been doing for quite a while, and we want it to stop now—at least in our home. We're sorry we have allowed this to continue for so long, but we've decided to make some changes. I see you've brought a six-pack of beer, but we're going to ask from now on that when you join us for dinner, you don't bring alcohol.
>
> We know you don't think that drinking a six-pack of beer affects you, but we feel it does. You come here sober, but by dessert you are slurring your words and are glassy-eyed. It's not healthy for the children to see you get drunk and to think this is acceptable behavior.
>
> We cannot tell you to stop drinking, although we wish you would consider doing that. We can, however, insist that when you are in our home, you will not drink alcohol. That includes tonight. You are welcome to stay for dinner but without the beer. I love you, Scott loves you, and the kids love you, Dad, but we don't love your drinking. You will always be welcome in our hearts, but you will not be welcome in our home when you drink. This is a new rule, and we are committed

to keeping it. Will you join us for dinner tonight and leave
the beer in your car?

Remember a critical point—you do not have to argue or defend
your boundary. It is what it is. This isn't up for negotiation with your
aging parent, so don't accept something like this: "How about instead
of drinking the entire six-pack, I'll just have three beers?" You've said
"no beer," and that means "no beer."

In a perfect world, Lisa's dad would respond, "Sure, honey," and
put the beer in his car, come back inside, and enjoy a wonderful eve-
ning. But alas, we do not live in a perfect world. That is why being
prepared is so important. Regardless of how your loved one may react,
don't let yourself be blindsided. Be ready to clearly and lovingly ver-
balize your response.

Also be ready to immediately follow through with your consequences, even if it's difficult to do so.

Had her dad pushed his way past and brushed-off her boundary,
Lisa was prepared to stand firm and insist that he leave their home,
followed by a call to her husband if he refused to go. Scott had a script
on his end, in case his father-in-law didn't take Lisa seriously.

All of this preparation entails a great deal of work—at first. If setting
boundaries and saying no were easy to do, we would have been doing
those things all along! Why have things gotten so out of hand? Why
have you spent time reading an entire book on how to set boundaries,
find sanity, and gain balance?

You are about to implement significant changes, and some of the
issues you are dealing with are quite serious. This isn't like telling a
coworker you're no longer going to cover for her extra long lunch
break. We're talking about establishing a new boundary in the relationship with your parents—one of the most important relationships
in your entire life.

Surely this relationship is worth the advanced planning—the extra
time and energy you expend to make sure you make your case effectively.
It's worth the effort of making sure you are indeed committed to the

new boundaries you are presenting. It's worth the work of considering all the consequences and making certain the transition happens with all the love, honor, respect, and dignity possible. Your relationship with your parents and your own health are both definitely worth it!

In some cases, you might be able to handle this transition with very little trouble. You might be able to verbally expose your new boundary quite easily. If that's your situation, praise God from whom all blessings flow!

Reaping the Rewards of Balance

Your ultimate goal is to mature—to live in sanity. You have charted a new course for your own life, and now your relationship with your parents is headed for new territory as well. You have spoken the truth in love. Things may be amazingly calm as everyone adjusts to this new world of accountability. You've done well to get this far, but you'll enjoy true success when you can consistently respond rationally to your parents when they react emotionally and test these new limits. Yes, your boundary declaration may precipitate a crisis that brings you to your knees.

If that happens, perhaps that is exactly where God has called you to be—on your knees before Him. Wendy Hamilton's response to my survey made this crystal clear:

> It is only God who is capable of loving child and parent wholly, completely, and perfectly. It is only His unfailing love that empowers us to respect the individuality He blessed us with when He created us unique and separate from our parents. His boundaries help us define our personal space and offer every sustainable resource we need to grow and become exactly who He designed us to be. When we were in our mother's womb, He knew us and generated hope-filled plans for us.
>
> Next to the verses that teach us how God gave His Son to us because He loved us, I think the most powerful verse in the Bible is this: "Speak the truth in love."
>
> When dealing with difficult people, we need to seek God's

peace at all cost. But I do not believe that the application of peace takes the form of harmony at all costs. Sometimes the only way to peace is to speak up. Going to God and relying on Him to strengthen us offers peace to us regardless of what our parents do or don't say or do.

Wendy's response powerfully summed up a key point in the Law of Exposure—the vital need to speak the truth in love. Cloud and Townsend encourage us that although the road may not be easy, there is still hope.

> When we begin to set boundaries with people we love, a really hard thing happens: they hurt. They may feel a hole where you used to plug up their aloneness, their disorganization, or their financial irresponsibility. Whatever it is, they will feel a loss.
>
> If you love them, this will be difficult for you to watch. But when you are dealing with someone who is hurting, remember that your boundaries are both necessary for you and helpful for them. If you have been enabling them to be irresponsible, your limit setting may nudge them toward responsibility.[2]

That is our prayer for our aging parents—that even in the midst of growing older, they may journey toward responsibility and accept the consequences of their actions. Yet the fact remains our parents have entered a new season in life as they become increasingly dependent on us and more responsibility rests on our shoulders. Knowing when to say yes and when to say no will weigh heavy on our hearts. We will constantly need to reassess when to address a stress trigger and when to let it go. The best way to know how to respond in any situation is to follow the *Y* step in SANITY and yield everything to God—to fully trust Him.

> And this is my prayer: that your love may abound more and more in knowledge and depth of insight.
>
> PHILIPPIANS 1:9

God willing, every step we take on this journey of setting boundaries brings us more knowledge and insight. It's important to learn to love in a healthy way, and adult children in pain who have had to set some very difficult boundaries often find that hard to do. Learning to love in a healthy way isn't always easy, but it's always God's way. God will meet us where we are, regardless of how broken or bitter we are. It doesn't matter where you are in your journey of setting boundaries with your aging parents. What matters is that you can stop the insanity right now—today—this very minute.

> Therefore we do not lose heart. Though outwardly we are wasting away, yet inwardly we are being renewed day by day. For our light and momentary troubles are achieving for us an eternal glory that far outweighs them all. So we fix our eyes not on what is seen, but on what is unseen. For what is seen is temporary, but what is unseen is eternal.
>
> 2 CORINTHIANS 4:16-18

You can gain sanity and begin an amazing adventure of self-discovery. When our priority becomes the development of an intimate relationship with Jesus, the sand in the hourglass of life shifts.

It's sometimes difficult to watch our aging parents navigate this road. We want so much to carry their burdens for them. The truth is, we *can* do many things for them without enabling—without damaging their dignity and causing anybody any emotional harm. We have more resources available today than ever before.

We need to be secure that whatever decisions we make are ours and are based on what we know and believe—on what God convicts us is right. Some say we should never say no to a parent—that setting boundaries in any form is dishonoring. Others say it's justifiable to disconnect totally from parents who refuse to change. Many would have us believe the only way to honor our aging parents when they become dependent is to take them into our own homes. Others say seniors should live in an environment that keeps them active and engaged with others their age.

Yes, it's true, we have much to consider as our parents grow older and more dependent on us for guidance. Yet the basis of our faith as Christians is always Jesus Christ Himself. We must abide in His truth. His truth will ultimately set us and our parents free.

When our priorities are aligned with God's and our relationship with Him is the heartbeat that sustains us, we are truly free. That is when we can begin to find sanity, set healthy boundaries, and authentically love our aging parents as He commands us.

23

A Closing Message from Allison

We can't get back the years we've lost. Yes, the Lord can redeem what the locust has eaten, but once our parents are gone from this earth, they are gone.

In my journey with my adult son, I have had to work very hard not to feel overwhelmed with guilt for the mistakes I made when he was young—and I made more than a few. Likewise, the years he spent in a drug-induced walking coma can never be replaced. Time is precious, and we have both wasted so much of it...yet there is still time left. We are working hard to restore our relationship and build something beautiful, strong, and new from the ashes. Our relationship is a work in progress, and I value every chance we have to strengthen our bond.

But until we meet in heaven, I'll never again have the opportunity to build a truly healthy relationship with my mother.

I recall when my son was a little boy, my mother often bought us groceries. Her food gifts were not extravagant or excessive, neither of us had a lot of money. Yet I would get so angry, we actually had fights about this. I saw this selfless act on her part as an insult to my ability to provide. I felt as if she didn't trust me to be responsible and take care of things. How wrong and foolish I was. In retrospect, I can see this was how she showed her love. She couldn't express it in words, but she showed it in countless ways. I wasn't able to see that back then—I wasn't able to see a great many things back then. Alas, I didn't always do the right thing.

If your parents are alive, you still have the opportunity to do the right thing. You can still make changes in your life that may strengthen or perhaps even restore your relationship with them. My prayer is that by setting healthy boundaries and finding sanity, you will discover how to love your aging parents in a more authentic way. And that God will grant you wisdom and peace as you guard your heart and the hearts of those you love.

One more thing, if I may…Many aging parents are not accustomed to openly showing emotion, and that can make it difficult for us as well. If this describes your mom or dad, I encourage you to break that cycle today. Take the initiative to tell your parents "I love you" while they can still hear you. They may or may not reciprocate, but I pray you'll take the chance and never regret it.

God's peace and blessings to you.

Allison

24

Sample Letters

Perhaps a face-to-face talk with your parents would not work in your situation. That is why I have included a few sample letters you can tweak and send. I've also included letters you could send to your spouse and siblings.

Diane Viere has helped me develop these letters. You may recall that Diane is the Director of Communications for the Setting Boundaries outreach, and she utilizes her skills to communicate directly with church and ministry leaders to introduce the international SANITY Support Group Network. Diane has a BS in psychology from Northwestern College, a Certificate in Christian Counseling, and she is a member of the American Association of Christian Counselors.

I have included six kinds of letters:

1. to a spouse who is well-meaning but unaware of boundary issues
2. to parents who are well-meaning but unaware of boundary issues
3. to parents whose boundaries you have overstepped
4. to parents who need to discuss their choices and preferences for the future

5. to parents who are toxic

6. to siblings who can help with aging parents

1. To a spouse who is well-meaning but unaware of boundary issues.

Dear _____,

Since I began caring for my parents, the dynamics of our marriage have been changing. I want to honor you and our history together, and I have begun to set healthy boundaries relating to the care of my parents. These boundaries will help me be proactive and feel more connected with the world, with our family, and with you.

I will begin by stopping some things. I want to stop my negative and emotional reactions to the stress triggers in my life. I want to be intentional in living and to stop being reactive. I want to stop giving our life away.

I want to stop the burnout we all are feeling and step back into balance. I have stopped believing that I do not have a choice in this matter, and I have started reminding myself of the difference between helping my parents and enabling them. This critical difference will influence the choices I make in the future.

I will stop believing I have to do it all and that I am the only person who can help my parents. I will stop reacting out of emotions stemming from fear, avoidance, denial, guilt, anger, shame, or myths. I want to stop my own negative behaviors so we can live life as God intended for us.

Will you be my accountability partner? Your support and encouragement will help me to stay strong when I feel weak. No one can do this alone, and I cherish the way you can help me by listening, discussing, and praying about the choices I will make in the future regarding my aging parents.

I love you.

2. To parents who are well-meaning but unaware of boundary issues.

Dear Mom and Dad,

I am so grateful for all that you have done for me. I have grown into the person I am today largely due to your influence and love. That is part of the reason I love you and want to help care for you.

Still, I am struggling to find balance in my life. The demands on me—a full-time job, three busy children, a wonderful marriage, and a life filled with so much to be grateful for—have left me feeling defeated. It is time to make a change.

I've been a little like an ostrich with my head in the sand, and it is time for a clearer view. I have been less than honest with you. Whenever you graciously ask me if I have time to do this or that, I almost always say yes, but then I feel resentment— not toward you, but toward myself for not being able to set healthy boundaries on my time and commitment.

I have promised myself that today I will begin to honor you, my family, and myself by setting healthy boundaries. I don't want to resent myself for the way I act with you. If for no other reason than that, beginning today, I commit to say what I mean and mean what I say. At times that might mean I will say no, and I want you to know when that happens that I am *not* rejecting you. I am simply setting a limit on the number of things I can say yes to.

I love you, Mom and Dad—and I mean that!

3. To parents whose boundaries you have overstepped.

Dear Mom and Dad,

I'm sorry I have been so demanding and impatient with you as we are making this life transition together. I've been looking for quick answers for the sudden changes that are occurring. As a result, I've overstepped your boundaries, and I've tried to make your decisions for you. That was wrong of me.

I'm so thankful you are my parents, and I love, honor and respect you. Yet I have been responding to your recent needs with fear and a lack of empathy. You have always been my heroes, but now you are experiencing changes in your health, finances, home, and independence. I have struggled to admit these transitions are necessary, and I've wondered what they must be like for you. If these losses are difficult for me, they must be even more difficult for you.

I've been learning about what setting healthy boundaries and the difference between helping and enabling. I now realize, that although I was trying to help you, I have disrespected you by acting as if you could not help yourself.

We don't always agree about what is best for you. But I have finally learned that I am not entitled to assume my way is best simply because I want what is best for you.

It's time to stop the disrespect. I want to honor you. It's time to stop burdening you with my contentious need to be right. I want to bless you. It's time to stop the animosity. I only want to love and appreciate who you have been and always will be to me—my mom and mad.

I love you. Thank you in advance for forgiving me.

4. To parents who need to discuss their choices and preferences for the future.

Dear Mom and Dad,

You've been going through quite a transition lately. I can only imagine how difficult it has been for you. Thank you for letting me help you.

Would it be possible for the three of us to have dinner and discuss some things that may be around the corner? As I continue to help you, I really want to make sure we do things according to your desires and wishes, and I'd like to hear what you have in mind.

At every transition in my life, you helped me plan and prepare, and you supported me through the scary times. Graduating from high school, going away to college, getting married, becoming a parent, moving for my job…I always felt secure knowing you were just a phone call away.

I want to support the decisions you have already made. I want to gently nudge you to continue making important decisions. You can count on me just as I have always been able to count on you. Sometimes talking with you about my future wasn't easy. I remember our conversation about sex during a family dinner when I was a teenager. Shiver me timbers—I didn't want to be there! But you guided me and challenged me to consider the physical and emotional consequences of my choices.

This family dinner may feel much like that one so long ago, and it is just as important. Will you help me by discussing your choices and preferences with me? Then I can help you follow through on these preparations by respectfully prioritizing your choices above any other considerations.

I love you.

5. *To parents who are toxic.*

Dear Mom and Dad,

How I wish I could magically wave a wand and make things better. I have felt so powerless as I have searched for just the right answers to change our contentious relationship.

I have taken a look at my role in our struggle. I have discovered that I have been trying to change everything and everyone else instead of changing my own behaviors. To strengthen my new discovery, I am determined to start doing these things:

- occasionally say no and never feel guilty for doing so
- take time for myself and my family without feeling selfish

- avoid dysfunctional conversations
- communicate with authenticity and respect
- show my respect for you and treat you like adults
- respect your decisions even when they're different from mine
- stop doing the things for you that you are capable of doing for yourself
- stop blaming you and accept responsibility for my choices
- say what I mean and mean what I say
- stop resenting our situation
- set healthy boundaries so I can help you when I can
- stop feeling responsible to fix everything and start looking for help

I love you, Mom and Dad, and I'm sorry for the part I have played in our drama. I no longer want to spend all of my energy on the negative; I want to spend my time caring for you in meaningful ways. I'm confident that in the long run, we'll all be happier that way.

6. To siblings who can help with aging parents.

Dear Brother and Sisters,

Well, this has certainly been a difficult season as I've tried to help Mom and Dad through this transition of care. I have stumbled through this process, and I need to ask your forgiveness.

Because Mom and Dad live closest to me, I assumed I was responsible for their care. I did not mean to exclude you from the joy of caring for our aging parents; I just made a response to an immediate and sudden need, and it seemed to make sense at the time. Please forgive me for excluding you in the loving care of Mom and Dad during this critical time.

Could we have a family meeting to discuss their needs and find a way to distribute the care required between all of us? Each of you has a specific skill set that is valuable to Mom and Dad. I'm sorry I have ignored this fact until now, and I would like to make some changes.

Let's talk.

Much love,

Notes

Part One: Avoiding Burnout and Building Mutual Respect

1. Henry Cloud and John Townsend, *Boundaries: When to Say Yes, When to Say No, to Take Control of Your Life* (Grand Rapids: Zondervan, 1992), 276.

2. Cloud and Townsend, *Boundaries*, 25.

3. Cloud and Townsend, *Boundaries*, 34.

4. Timothy S. Smick, ed., *Eldercare for the Christian Family* (Dallas: W Publishing Group, 1990), 6.

5. Administration on Aging, "Aging Statistics," www.aoa.gov/aoaroot/Aging_Statistics/index.aspx.

6. National Alliance for Caregiving and American Association of Retired Persons, *Caregiving in the U.S.* (April 2004). www.caregiving.org/data/04finalreport.pdf.

7. Cloud and Townsend, *Boundaries*, 285.

Chapter 1: The Road to Burnout

1. Chesley B. Sullenberger, "What I Got Back," *Parade Magazine*, October 11, 2009. Adapted from Chesley B. Sullenberger and Jeffrey Zaslow, *Highest Duty: My Search for What Really Matters* (New York: HarperCollins, 2009).

2. Cloud and Townsend, *Boundaries*, 129.

3. Cloud and Townsend, *Boundaries*, 129-30.

4. Cloud and Townsend, *Boundaries*, 103.

5. Virelle Kidder, *Meet Me at the Well: Take a Month and Water Your Soul* (Chicago: Moody, 2008), 21.

6. Kidder, *Meet Me at the Well*, 20.

7. David Hawkins, *Dealing with the CrazyMakers in Your Life: Setting Boundaries on Unhealthy Relationships* (Eugene: Harvest House, 2007), 26.

8. Jane Bluestein, *Parents, Teens and Boundaries: How to Draw the Line* (Deerfield Beach: Health Communications, 1993), 7-8.

9. Bluestein, *Parents, Teens and Boundaries*, 8-9.

10. Cloud and Townsend, *Boundaries*, 84.

11. Cloud and Townsend, *Boundaries*, 83.

Chapter 2: Stop the Insanity!

1. See Cloud and Townsend, *Boundaries,* 29.
2. Max Lucado, *Grace for the Moment: Inspirational Thoughts for Each Day of the Year* (Nashville: Countryman, 2000), 21.
3. Cloud and Townsend, *Boundaries*, 132.
4. Kim Thomas, *Even God Rested: Why It's Okay for Women to Slow Down* (Eugene: Harvest House, 2003), 44.
5. Cloud and Townsend, *Boundaries*, 132.

Chapter 3: It's All About Change and Choice

1. Lucado, *Grace for the Moment*, 36.
2. Dr. Laura Schlessinger, *Bad Childhood—Good Life: How to Blossom and Thrive in Spite of an Unhappy Childhood* (Harper Collins, 2006), 2.
3. Schlessinger, *Bad Childhood—Good Life*, 23-24.
4. Hawkins, *Dealing with the CrazyMakers in Your Life*, 205.

Chapter 4: "I'm Only Trying to Help!"

1. Cloud and Townsend, *Boundaries*, 25.
2. Betty Benson Robertson, *Changing Places: A Christian's Guide to Caring for Aging Parents* (Kansas City: Beacon Hill Press, 2002), 13.

Chapter 5: The Motivation Behind the Madness

1. Schlessinger, *Bad Childhood—Good Life*, 7.
2. Cloud and Townsend, *Boundaries*, 90.
3. Mark Sichel, *Healing from Family Rifts: Ten Steps to Finding Peace After Being Cut Off from a Family Member* (New York: McGraw-Hill, 2004), 41.
4. Florence Littauer, *Personality Plus: How to Understand Others by Understanding Yourself* (Grand Rapids: Fleming H. Revell, 1983), 11.
5. Littauer, *Personality Plus*, 12.
6. Littauer, *Personality Plus,* 14.
7. Littauer, *Personality Plus,* 172.
8. Sichel, *Healing from Family Rifts*, 44.
9. Cloud and Townsend, *Boundaries*, 92.

Chapter 6: Pain from the Past

1. Ray Pritchard, *The Healing Power of Forgiveness: Let Go of Your Hurt, Experience Renewed Relationships, and Find New Intimacy with God* (Eugene: Harvest House, 2005), 47.
2. Robertson, *Changing Places*, 65.
3. Schlessinger, *Bad Childhood—Good Life,* 14.

Chapter 7: Toxic Elders and Destructive Choices

1. Sichel, *Healing from Family Rifts*, 43.
2. Sichel, *Healing from Family Rifts,* 43.

Chapter 8: The Power of Love and Forgiveness

1. Stormie Omartian, *Seven Prayers That Will Change Your Life Forever* (Nashville: J. Countryman, 2006).
2. Phil McGraw, "Make a Conscious Decision to Appreciate Yourself Every Single Day," *O: The Oprah Magazine*, November 2009, 68-70.
3. Lucado, *Grace for the Moment*, 29.

Chapter 9: Respect

1. Pritchard, *The Healing Power of Forgiveness*, 135.
2. Cloud and Townsend, *Boundaries*, 83.

Chapter 10: When Your Parents Become Dependent

1. Smick, *Eldercare for the Christian Family*, 13.
2. Smick, *Eldercare for the Christian Family*, 57.
3. Smick, *Eldercare for the Christian Family*, 199.
4. Smick, *Eldercare for the Christian Family*, 10.

Chapter 11: Financial Fallout

1. Cloud and Townsend, *Boundaries*, 125-26.

Chapter 12: S—Stop Your Own Negative Behavior

1. Leslie Vernick, *The Emotionally Destructive Relationship: Seeing It, Stopping It, Surviving It* (Eugene: Harvest House, 2007), 119-20.
2. Allison Bottke, *Setting Boundaries with Your Adult Children* (Eugene, OR: Harvest House, 105).
3. Bottke, *Setting Boundaries with Your Adult Children*, 106-7.

Chapter 14: N—Nip Excuses in the Bud

1. Cloud and Townsend, *Boundaries*, 228.

Chapter 15: I—Implement Rules and Boundaries

1. Cloud and Townsend, *Boundaries*, 100-101.

Chapter 16: T—Trust Your Instincts

1. Bottke, *Setting Boundaries with Your Adult Children*, 139-40.

Chapter 17: *Y*—Yield Everything to God

1. Vernick, *The Emotionally Destructive Relationship*, 197.

2. Vernick, *The Emotionally Destructive Relationship*, 198.

Part Three: The Dawn of a New Beginning

1. Bottke, *Setting Boundaries with Your Adult Children*, 154-55.

Chapter 21: Consequences

1. Bluestein, *Parents, Teens and Boundaries*, 9-10.

2. Hawkins, *Dealing with the CrazyMakers in Your Life*, 210-11.

3. Cloud and Townsend, *Boundaries*, 38.

4. Hawkins, *Dealing with the CrazyMakers in Your Life*, 210.

5. Sichel, *Healing from Family Rifts,* 61.

6. Schlessinger, *Bad Childhood—Good Life,* 47.

7. Cloud and Townsend, *Boundaries*, 240.

8. Cloud and Townsend, *Boundaries*, 41.

Chapter 22—Sowing and Reaping

1. Cloud and Townsend, *Boundaries*, 278.

2. Cloud and Townsend, *Boundaries*, 249.

Stay in Touch

I care about you and your journey. Please send an e-mail or drop me a note to share your SANITY experience. Visit the Setting Boundaries website to find out more about the Six Steps to SANITY and 12 Weeks to Freedom sessions currently meeting online or at a location near you.

www.settingboundaries.com
Allison@SettingBoundaries.com

Allison Bottke
Setting Boundaries
4749 Misty Ridge Drive
Fort Worth, TX 76137-5103

About the Author

Allison Bottke is a bestselling inspirational author and speaker and the founder of the acclaimed God Allows U-Turns© book series and outreach ministry. She is the author or editor of more than 24 books. Allison Bottke Ministries encompasses multiple outreach organizations. Visit Allison's website at:

www.AllisonBottke.com

Allison has also developed the Setting Boundaries outreach, including the SANITY Support Group Network, which has groups meeting around the world. For more information visit www.settingboundaries.com. She also writes contemporary fiction for baby-boomer women, including a new trilogy series called Va Va Va Boom! Find out more at www.Boomer BabesRock.com.

You can also find SANITY in the first of
Allison's Setting Boundaries books…

Setting Boundaries with Your Adult Children

If your adult children make life painful for you, this important landmark book from the creator of the successful God Allows U-Turns © series provides you with hope, help, and a process for healing.

Writing from firsthand experience, Allison identifies the lies that kept her and her son in bondage—and how she overcame them. Additional real life stories from other parents are woven throughout the text.

A new kind of tough-love book that empowers you with a proactive approach for your challenging relationships with adult children, *Setting Boundaries with Your Adult Children* outlines the Six Steps to SANITY:

> *S*—Stop enabling, stop blaming yourself, and stop the flow of money.
>
> *A*—Assemble a support group.
>
> *N*—Nip excuses in the bud.
>
> *I*—Implement rules and boundaries.
>
> *T*—Trust your instincts.
>
> *Y*—Yield everything to God.

Foreword by Carol Kent, author of *When I Lay My Isaac Down*.

Six Steps to SANITY Support Groups
An Invitation from Allison

If you have found the Six Steps to SANITY helpful in your journey to set healthy boundaries, I'd like to personally invite you to make a SANITY Support Group available in your community. We have groups meeting around the country, but we need more people like you to help us bring this life-changing support group program to the people who need it. We've made it easy to coordinate and facilitate a group, and we'll give you hands-on support every step of the way. We have flyers, public service announcements (PSA) for local TV and radio stations, and a press release for your local newspaper. We even have glossy color brochures you can distribute. We'll gladly send you a stack of brochures free of charge.

Please visit our website to find out more about the Setting Boundaries outreach. We've tried to make this site as comprehensive as possible. In addition to offering our 12-week program online, we also conduct periodic live webcasts and special events to help reinforce the Six Steps to SANITY. Check out the What's New page for frequent updates. You can also subscribe to *SANITY Now!* and participate in our community forum. And don't miss the theatrical videos on our site that dramatically depict boundary-setting scenarios. Additionally, our online storefront has study guides and support group materials. Please stop by today. And share this valuable resource with a friend in need—you may change a life.

www.SettingBoundaries.com

What People Are Saying About SANITY Support Groups

"We are different people than we were before we started the Six Steps to SANITY and 12 Weeks to Freedom program. We've grown in our understanding of our boundaries and responsibilities with our two adult boys. We have more peace and control in our lives now that we are not taking responsibility for their lives. Our new boundaries were initially met with anger and disappointment, but both our boys have grown as we've communicated our boundaries. Thank you for bringing this freedom into our lives and hearts."

"Our SANITY Support Group has brought an incredible amount of freedom to each participant in our group. None of us believed we could ever escape the 'gerbil wheel' of chaos and confusion when we first began meeting, but believe it or not, after week one, we were all motivated by the relief we felt to return each week and begin to implement the Six Steps to SANITY. One participant actually drives more than three hours to meet with us! God is so good, and we are grateful that you have written this book and developed the SANITY Support Group Network for such a time as this."

"The online SANITY Support Group has brought such freedom to my life. Life with my adult child is still throwing me a lot of curve-balls, but I'm finding that with SANITY, I'm a pretty good catch. I'm much stronger than I ever imagined I could be. Thank you for supporting my journey to sanity!"

"We have been having very good SANITY Support Group meetings with lots of sharing. We feel certain the Six Steps to SANITY are helping us; we no longer feel like we are on the merry-go-round, wondering what we should do next for our adult son. The Six Steps to SANITY Support Group Network has freed us (and our group members) from so much pain; thank you for showing us the way out of the 'dark night of our souls.'"

**Book #3 in the acclaimed
Setting Boundaries series by Allison Bottke**

*Setting Boundaries with Difficult People:
Six Steps to SANITY*

Are there difficult people in your life who seem to bring chaos, crisis, and drama into any space they occupy—particularly your space?

Are you struggling with poor choices other people are making? Are you turned inside out and living from one challenging situation to the next in pain, fear, anger, or frustration because of their choices? Can you answer "yes" to one or more of the following questions?

- Do people take advantage of you?
- Do you have trouble saying "no"?
- Do you suffer from feelings of guilt much of the time?
- Do you feel as though you have no control over your life?
- Do you try to have too much control over your life?

Whether it's a situation concerning a spouse, in-law, boss, co-worker, family member, neighbor, or friend, if you have allowed others to overstep your boundaries and make you insane, it's time to set healthy boundaries and take back your life—it's time to find SANITY now.

We can and should set healthy boundaries with difficult people. Yet too often, we ignore the need to do so because of fear of being misunderstood, and we simply wait passively, letting the chips fall where they may. We are then put in the position of having to continually put out fires instead of preventing them. *If only we could change the difficult people in our lives!*

Could it be the problem isn't that we have difficult people in our lives... but in how we respond to them?

If you have a challenging relationship with a difficult person, *Setting Boundaries with Difficult People* will help you learn how to identify if a lack of healthy boundaries could be the cause. It will help you learn that setting boundaries is a form of protection—for both parties. It's a way to stay on alert and face problems early on, so that nothing will be allowed to fester to the point it destroys your life, your peace-of-mind, your sanity.

Even more important, *Setting Boundaries with Difficult People* will give you the tools needed to change your life.

Discover the truth that over 60,000 readers have come to learn;

Six Steps to SANITY can transform your life!

Allison Bottke's acronym **SANITY** provides a memorable description for her successful six-step program that will help you take back your life and find SANITY in seemingly out-of-control situations.

> S = Stop your own negative behavior
> A = Assemble a support group
> N = Nip excuses in the bud
> I = Implement rules and boundaries
> T = Trust your instincts
> Y = Yield everything to God

Setting Boundaries with Difficult People isn't just a book to address a cultural epidemic—our growing inability as a society to set healthy boundaries—it's a ministry designed to inspire, empower, and equip men and women with the tools to transform lives.

Founded by Allison Bottke and based on the Setting Boundaries book series published by Harvest House Publishers, you can find out more about the **Six Steps to SANITY** and the international **SANITY Support Group Network** by visiting Allison's websites:

www.AllisonBottkeMinistries.com
www.SettingBoundaries.com

Allison Bottke's Setting Boundaries *books offer sound psychological advice that is stunningly integrated with the importance of understanding that God is the ultimate authority, overriding both societal and psychological beliefs.*
–Mark Sichel, author of *Healing from Family Rifts: Ten Steps to Finding Peace After Being Cut Off from a Family Member*